Steps to

English Composition

BOOK I

TOM THUMB ESSAYS

H. MARTIN

M.A. (Oxon.), O.B.E.

Revised by Editorial Board

S. Chand & Company Pvt. Ltd., New Delhi

BLACKIE

ELT BOOKS

BLACKIE

BLACKIE ELT BOOKS
(An imprint of S. Chand Publishing)
A Division of S. Chand And Company Limited
(An ISO 9001 Certified Company)
7361, Ram Nagar, Qutab Road, New Delhi-110055
Phone: 23672080-81-82, 9899107446, 9911310888; Fax: 91-11-23677446
www.schandpublishing.com; e-mail : helpdesk@schandpublishing.com

Branches :

Ahmedabad : Ph: 27541965, 27542369, ahmedabad@schandpublishing.com
Bengaluru : Ph: 22268048, 22354008, bangalore@schandpublishing.com
Bhopal : Ph: 4274723, 4209587, bhopal@schandpublishing.com
Chandigarh : Ph: 2625356, 2625546, 4025418, chandigarh@schandpublishing.com
Chennai : Ph: 28410027, 28410058, chennai@schandpublishing.com
Coimbatore : Ph: 2323620, 4217136, coimbatore@schandpublishing.com (Marketing Office)
Cuttack : Ph: 2332580, 2332581, cuttack@schandpublishing.com
Dehradun : Ph: 2711101, 2710861, dehradun@schandpublishing.com
Guwahati : Ph: 2738811, 2735640, guwahati@schandpublishing.com
Hyderabad : Ph: 27550194, 27550195, hyderabad@schandpublishing.com
Jaipur : Ph: 2219175, 2219176, jaipur@schandpublishing.com
Jalandhar : Ph: 2401630, 5000630, jalandhar@schandpublishing.com
Kochi : Ph: 2809208, 2808207, cochin@schandpublishing.com
Kolkata : Ph: 23353914, 23357458, kolkata@schandpublishing.com
Lucknow : Ph: 4026791, 4065646, lucknow@schandpublishing.com
Mumbai : Ph: 22690881, 22610885, mumbai@schandpublishing.com
Nagpur : Ph: 6451311, 2720523, 2777666, nagpur@schandpublishing.com
Patna : Ph: 2300489, 2302100, patna@schandpublishing.com
Pune : Ph: 64017298, pune@schandpublishing.com
Raipur : Ph: 2443142, raipur@schandpublishing.com (Marketing Office)
Ranchi : Ph: 2361178, ranchi@schandpublishing.com
Sahibabad : Ph: 2771235, 2771238, delhibr-sahibabad@schandpublishing.com

By arrangement with MANECKJI COOPER EDUCATION TRUST, Mumbai
Fourteenth Edition 1996
Revised and Enlarged Edition 2015
First Impression 2019

ISBN : 978-81-219-0735-4 **Product Code :** SCS2SEC010ENGAB16MLN

PRINTED IN INDIA

By Nirja Publishers & Printers Pvt. Ltd., 54/3/2, Jindal Paddy Compound, Kashipur Road, Rudrapur-263153, Uttarakhand and published by S Chand And Company Limited, 7361, Ram Nagar, New Delhi -110 055.

PREFACE

These miniature or "Tom Thumb" essays have been written for younger children who are just beginning to do a bit of English composition. They are, therefore, very short, and are written in a very simple language. They are not made to be copied or learnt by heart, but are intended as models for short essays or paragraph-writing; for they may be regarded either as tiny essays or short single paragraphs. To prevent mere parrot-like copying, the teacher can give one of the essays to be read and studied, and then set an essay to be written on a different but similar subject. For example, the essay on '**The Tiger**' or '**The Lion**' could be read as a model for an essay on '**The Bear**'; the essay on '**The Carpenter**' would serve as a model for one on '**The Tailor**'; and an essay on "**Waste Not, Want Not**" could be written on the model of the essay on '**Thrift**'; and so on. These tiny essays are too short to be divided into paragraphs, each being itself an average paragraph; but the line of thought in each can easily be detected. The Essays have not been classified as Descriptive Essays, Reflective Essays and Biographical Essays. However, half of the total number are descriptive (mainly of common objects), this type of essay is the easiest for children. Some fifty are Reflective, on general subjects. Proverbs form good subjects for this type of essay, and some are included. The smallest number are Biographical.

For the writing of a biographical essay some special knowledge of the subject is needed; and this may be supplied to the class by the teacher in the shape of a short talk.

Publishers

Hints on Writing Little Essays

Even a tiny essay cannot be written without thought and planning. Before it can be written, some line of thought must be decided upon. So, follow these steps :

1. First think over your subject to see what you can say about it. As ideas come into your mind, jot them down briefly on a bit of paper.
2. Next, arrange these ideas in some logical order; that is, make an outline. For example, study Essay No. 82 on "**Discipline**". You will find it is made up of three ideas. The outline of this essay would be :-
   (a) Discipline in learning to obey rules.
   (b) The discipline of a society, as in a school, games and an army;
   (c) Self-discipline or learning self-control.
3. Remember the essay you are to write is to be **very short**, about **150 words**. So you cannot give more than two or three short sentences to each point. Say as much as you can in as few words as possible.
4. Revise your essay carefully when you have written it, to see if you can make it **clear, simple** and **short**.

H. Martin

CONTENTS

1. A Bazaar

The bazaar is a narrow street of few houses and shops. The shops are all open to the street. The shopkeepers sit inside, with their goods all round them. There are sweet-shops. The fruit-shops are piled up with bananas, mangoes, melons and oranges. The grocery shops are bounded with heaps of grain, rice, lentils and species. The tailors sit cross-legged, cutting and sewing. Brass-workers hammer the brass items. Silver-smiths make bangles. Rich carpet-merchants sit smoking their *hookahs*. The bazaar is crowded with people. They buy and sell, talk and shout. It is hot, dusty, smelly, and very noisy. Animals like bullocks, camels pass along with jangling bells. Crows caw, monkeys chatter, and children shout in their play. Ash-covered fakirs beg from the shops. A Brahmani bull takes what he wants without asking. A temple bell rings, or a harsh conch-shell blows. All is noise and bustle.

2. A Bullock-Cart

The Indian bullock-cart is heavy and clumsy. It is made all of wood. It has thick wooden wheels, with no springs. It crawls slowly along the road, drawn by two bullocks, or a buffalo. It is loaded with corn, *hay* or sugarcane. Its heavy wheels creak as it jolts over the ruts in the road. The man who drives it sits on the pole in front. Or he lolls on the top of the load half-asleep. Now and then he wakes up to see the bullocks, or them pat. The bullocks do not go any faster. Neither the driver nor the bullocks are ever in hurry. They get there some time. The bullock-cart is very old-fashioned. It is very much like the carts used in India a hundred years ago. In the same way the farmers then took their stuff to the market place.

3. A Fakir (Sadhus)

Some fakirs are holy men; but most are idle hobos. Naga fakir goes about naked. Fakirs wear no clothes except a small loin-cloth. His hair is long and greasy. He covers his body with ashes. He looks dirty, and never seems to wash himself. He carries a long bamboo, or an iron stick with a ring fastened to it. He also has a begging-bowl, made of brass or the hard skin of a gourd. He sits by the roadside, begging and muttering prayers. People passing by put food or coins into his bowl. Fakirs are often seen in the bazaars. They pass along in front of the shops. They do not ask for food or money. They have no need to do that. The shopkeepers put rice and dal and milk into their bowls. They are afraid that the fakirs will curse them if they do not give them anything.

4. The Farmer

The Indian farmer is a simple villager. He may not be able to read or write, but he knows his job. He knows his land, and he knows how to get good crops from it. A farmer's work is different at different times of the year. In the rainy season he ploughs his fields. Then he plants maize, or cotton, or sugar-cane, for the *Kharif* crop. The crops are reaped in September or October. Then he ploughs again, and sows wheat for the *rabi* harvest. This is reaped in March or April threshed and winnowed. The hot, dry weather then begins. Nothing can be done on the land. But the farmer still has to look after his cows, sheep and goats. In June, with the rains, the year's work begins again. So the farmer lives simple but works hard for healthy and useful crops.

5. A Villager's Day

The Indian villager is there "early to bed and early to rise". He is up at dawn, and goes to bed soon after sunset. He first has his early morning tea or milk and roti. Then he milks the cows, and sends them out to graze. He then goes to the fields for his day's work—ploughing, weeding, sowing, watering or reaping. At noon his wife or daughter brings him his midday meal. He eats it in the shade of a tree. Then he may rest a bit, if it is hot. He works on till sunset. Then he walks over the fields back to his village. After his evening meal, he sits a while chatting with his friends and smoking his hookah. In the summer they sit under the village tree. In the winter they sit round a fire. Soon after dark, he is in bed and asleep. So goes his daily life.

6. The Carpenter

A carpenter works with wood. He makes wooden chairs, tables, beds and almirahs for the house. He makes wooden carts and ploughs for the farmers. When a house is being built, the carpenter makes the wooden doors and window-frames. A carpenter must have a lot of tools. He has saws for sawing wood into pieces, and sharp chisels and axes to cut it. He uses a plane to make the wood smooth. He fastens pieces of wood together with his hammer and nails. A carpenter is a skilled workman. It takes a long time to learn to do the work properly. A carpenter has to learn how to use his tools. He has to know what can be done with wood. He has to think about his work, and plan it out. In India this has been seen that the son of a carpenter generally becomes a carpenter. He is taught by his father.

7. The Mason

A mason works in stone. He is really a stone-cutter. The mason cuts and shapes the stones for building a wall or a house. But masons also do general building work. They mix mortar and lay bricks. They plaster the walls and roof with mortar and cement. They make floors of cement or stone. So a mason is not only a stone-cutter, but also a builder. A mason has different kinds of tools for his work. He uses a very large and strong saw for cutting large pieces of stone. This saw is worked by two men. Then he uses hammers and chisels for shaping and smoothing the stone. He has spades for mixing mortar and cement; trowels for laying mortar on bricks; hods for carrying bricks and stone; and flat wooden tools for smoothing plaster. So the work of a mason is skilled. It takes a long time to learn it.

8. The Blacksmith

A man who works in metal is called a "smith". A copper-smith works in copper; a gold-smith works in gold; a silver-smith works in silver; a tin-smith works in tin. But a smith who works in iron is called a "blacksmith". The chief work of a blacksmith is to make horse-shoes and to shoe horses. His workshop is called a smithy. It has a big fire, blown up by bellows, called a forge. This is how he makes a horse-shoe. He puts a piece of iron into the forge till it is redhot. Then he takes it out with a pair of tongs. He then lays it on a heavy block of iron called an anvil. He then beats it into shape with a splash of water, to make it cold. He fastens the shoe to the horse's hoof with nails. The blacksmith does other kinds of iron-work as well.

9. The Washerman (Dhobi)

In England women wash the clothes. They soak them first in hot soapy water. Then they rub them with soap till they are clean. They hang them out to dry in the sun on a clothes-line. In India men do the washing. A washerman is called a "dhobi". The *dhobi* washes clothes in a different way. He stands in the water at the edge of a tank or river. Before him is a big flat stone. He wets the dirty clothes in the cold water and applies soap. Then he beats them on the stone. He rinses them out in the water. He then spreads them out on the bank to dry. The *dhobi* often tears clothes on the hard stone, and breaks buttons. But on the whole he washes well. He has a bicycle to carry the clothes, those he washes. The *dhobi* earns his living by hard work. He does not get very much for his toil. These days generally people use washing machine to wash the clothes.

10. The Postman

You write a letter to a friend in a far-off town. How does it get to him? First, you post it. Then a postman opens the post-box, and takes your letter to the post-office. There it is put into a bag with other letters going to the same place. The bag of letters is taken to a railway station. It is put into a train going to your friend's town. The bag is taken out at the station of that town. It is taken to the post office. There the letters are sorted and given to different postmen. One postman gets your letter in his bag. He takes it to your friend's house. Your friend gets your letter and reads it. So you see a postman is the first and last link in a long chain between you and your friend. One postman collects your letter. Another postman gives it to your friend. Present days emails, SMS and cell phones have shorten the postman's work.

11. The Policeman

It may seem strange that people will obey a single policeman. He puts up his hand, and motor-cars and carriages stop at once. He takes up a thief, and the thief goes with him quietly. Why is this? It is because the single policeman has all the powers of the law behind him. People are not afraid of him; they are afraid of the law which he stands for. So a few unarmed policeman can keep order, and keep us and our houses safe. The police have to keep order. They see that the laws are obeyed. They try to find out crimes, and take up criminals. They protect our lives and property. They also look after the traffic in city streets. A policeman carries is his "truncheon". A truncheon is a stout, heavy stick. But he does not often use it.

12. The Gardener

The Bible says that Adam, the first man, was a gardener. So a gardener belongs to the oldest trade in the world. A gardener must have a lot of knowledge. He must know about plants: how they grow and what they are good for. He must know a lot about soils, and how to mix them to suit different plants. He must know the seasons of the year—when to sow, when the flowers will come. And he must know the signs of the weather—when it is going to be hot or cold, dry or rainy. A gardener needs patience. He must learn to wait for his plants to grow, flower and fruit. He needs foresight, too. He must be able to look ahead, and plan for the changing seasons. He must be hard-working; for a gardener's work is heavy. And he must be regular in his work.

13. The Cow

Everybody knows what a cow looks like. But there are different kinds of cows. The Indian cow is a small animal, with a hump on its back. The English or American cows are big in size. An American cow gives many times milk. The cow is very useful to us. It gives us milk and milk is a perfect food. Milk is the only food a baby can in take; and children live mostly on milk. Grown-up people could not live without milk too. From milk we make butter and cheese. Good butter is made from the rich cream on the top of the milk. Butter is a very good food. Ghee is made with melted butter; and ghee is used in most Indian dishes. Cheese, too, is a wholesome food, and it is nice to taste. So we get three kinds of good milk food from the cow—milk-shake, butter and cheese.

14. The Horse

Horses were at first wild animals. They lived in herds, moving about in search of pasture. But they have been tamed by men for thousands of years. Horses are used for riding, and for drawing carts and carriages. Before the days of trains and motor-cars, people used horses for riding and making long journeys. The horse is useful to us because of its strength, its speed and its cleverness. The horse is very strong. It can trot and gallop for a long way. It can go very fast. And it is clever. It can be trained to know what is wanted of it. The horse is indeed a noble creature. It is beautiful to look at. It is willing and obedient. A good master comes to love his horse. And a good horse loves its master. Next to the dog, the horse is the friend of a man kind.

15. The Donkey

The poor donkey is often badly treated. People think it is a foolish animal. Yet the donkey is not as foolish as it looks. It may not be clever like a dog or a horse; but it is not fool. It does well whatever the work one want from it. Donkeys are useful animals. They are used mostly for carrying loads. We can see that donkeys carry soil, bricks, pots and pans. In some countries, like Egypt and Persia, the donkeys are honoured. Chiefs and sheikhs that it is fine to ride on white asses. The donkeys. It takes bad treatment very quietly. But it is obstinate. It does not make much fuss, but quietly tries to go its own way.

16. The Dog

Dogs are very clever animals. They can be trained to do many kinds of useful work. Some make good watch-dogs. In cold countries dogs are trained to drag sledges over the snow. Dogs are used in hunting, like foxhounds, greyhounds and deerhounds. The famous St. Bernard dogs are taught to search for and save travellers lost in the snow on the Alps. The cleverest kind of dog is the sheep-dog. A good sheep-dog can look after a flock of sheep almost as well as the shepherd. There are many kinds of dogs. Most of them are useful for something. The dog is called the friend of man.. Many dog owners feel they are real friends. Dogs learn to love their masters. They will follow them everywhere. They will often defend their masters at the cost of their own lives. Some dogs have even died of grief when their masters died.

17. The Cat

People keep cats as pets. Cats are pretty animals, covered with soft fur. They are of different colours. Some are black, some white, some grey, some brown. Kittens, or young cats, are very playful. They play for hours with little balls, fallen leaves, or bits of string. The main use of cats is to catch mice and rats. Like their big cousins tigers, cats can be seen in the dark. They hunt for mice at night. Mice are a great pest in a house. Either the kill them, or drove them away. Cats have been tamed for thousands of years. They are kept as pets in ancient Egypt. Cats are very different from dogs. Dogs love persons, but cats love places. A dog follow his master anywhere. But a cat loves the comfort of the house, and stays at home. Its love is what we call "cupboard love."

18. The Rat

Rats and mice are cousins. Both are great thieves. Rats live in towns and villages. There they can find much food. They hide in holes and drains in the day-time. They come out at night to steal. Rats destroy large amounts of grain and other kinds of food every year. In India, rats are very dangerous. They carry the plague-flea which gives people plague. The only way to keep plague away is to kill the rats. So men are always at war with rats. There are different ways of catching and killing rats. They can be caught in traps. Cats and dogs are good rat eaters. They can catch and kill a lot. Every ship carries hundreds of rats. This is the way rats have spread all over the world. Some say they first came from China.

19. The Monkey

A monkey is like a man in shape. But it has a tail, and four hands. Monkeys are tree animals. They climb the trees easily with their four hands. They live most of the time up in the trees and can jump from one tree to another. In this way they will travel for miles in the forest over the trees. They sleep at night high up in the trees. Monkeys feed on nuts, berries and fruits. They often steal fruits from orchards. Monkeys are very curious. When they notice anything new, they want to know all about it. So they can easily be caught in traps. Monkeys are great mimics. They like to copy what they see men do. So tame monkeys can be taught to do funny tricks. One kind of monkey is called an ape. So the word "ape" means to copy or mimic.

20. The Elephant

The elephant is the largest of all animals. It is a strange animal to look at. It has thick legs, huge sides and back, large ears, small eyes, a short tail, and great white tusks. Its long nose, or trunk, is the strangest thing about it. It uses its trunk like a hand. It picks things up with its trunk, and puts them into its mouth. It sucks up water with its trunk, and squirts it into its mouth for drinking. Elephants are very strong. And they are very clever. Elephants are useful animals. They are trained to draw heavy loads. They are taught to carry logs of wood on their tusks, and pile them up in perfect order. They are also used in hunting tigers in the jungle. In early years they were used in battle. Kings and Nawabs were used to ride on elephants in state processions.

21. The Camel

The camel is a big animal of two kinds. One has two humps on its back; it is called the Bactrian camel. The other has one hump; it is called the Arabian camel. The camel is called "ship of the desert". Why? Because, as people cross the sea by ships, similarly, a desert can be crossed only with the help of camels. Camels can go a long time with very little food or drink. How can they do this? They carry stores of water in their stomach, and much fat in their "humps". A fasting camel is really feeding on its hump. The camel is also very strong, and can go on day after day without getting tired. So it can make long journeys over the hot, dry sandy deserts. It is a fine sight to see a line of camels marching in a caravan. They hold their heads up proudly, and tread steadily on.

22. The Tiger

The tiger is a savage and cruel animal. We say, "As cruel as a tiger". It is really a great cat. In fact, it is a large, strong and fine-looking animal. Its fur is yellow, marked with black stripes. It is shaped like a cat, with a long tail, round head and thick padded feet. It has sharp claws and strong teeth. The tiger is an Indian animal. There are many in the jungles of Bengal. Like cats, tigers hunt at night. They kill big animals, like deer, cows, sheep and goats. They also attack men. Some become "man-eaters". They like to eat men flesh very much. Tigers are feared by farmers. They come at night to steal their sheep and cows. We should protect our tigers from the hunters.

23. The Lion

The lion is called the King of Beasts. It looks like a king. It has golden mane on its neck, and holds its head up proudly. The lion stands for courage. We say a brave man is like a lion, or has the heart of a lion. But the lion is not really very brave. It would fight when attacked. But it will not attack a man. It will get away if it can. The lion is a big cat. It hunts at night. It can be seen in the dark. Lions kill and eat big animals, like wild deer. They are feared by farmers in Africa, for they steal their cows and sheep. Once there were many lions in India; but now there are only a few in the Gir forest of Saurashtra. Lions are largely found in the forests of Africa.

24. The Whale

The whale is the largest sea creature. A full-grown whale may be forty feet long. It is round and fat, and looks very huge. The whale lives in the sea; but it is not a fish. It is a sea animal. Whales cannot breathe in the water like fishes. They have to come up to breathe. They blow out the water, like a big fountain, and breathe. Then they sink down again under the sea. Whales are hunted for their oil, called "whale oil". Hunting the whale is called "whaling". It is a hard and dangerous job. Ships go into the northern seas to seek for whales. A whale is caught with a "harpoon". A harpoon is a very heavy kind of spear. It is fastened to a long rope. The harpoon is thrown at the whale. It sticks into it. The whale tries to get away. But it is held by the rope.

25. Snakes

Snakes are common in India. We know them well. There are many kinds of snakes. The Boas and Pythons are one kind. These are very large snakes. One may be thirty feet long, and as thick as a man's thigh. They are not poisonous. They kill their victims by crushing them to death. The biggest of this kind are found in African forests. Some snakes are quite harmless, like the Indian Rock-snake. But many snakes are very poisonous. In India we have the Cobra, the Krait, Russel's Viper, and many more. The bite of these snakes mean death. Thousands of people are killed every year in India by snake-bite. Snakes do not sting, they bite. A snake has two hollow teeth, called "fangs". Each fang rests on a little bag of poison. When the snake bites, the fangs are pressed back on these bags. The liquid poison is squirted into the wound.

26. The Frog

The frog begins its life in an egg. Frog's eggs look like little balls of white jelly. They float in the water of ponds in the spring. These eggs are hatched in a fortnight. Tiny little black creatures, like wee fishes, come out. These soon become larger. They look like round black heads with tails. They are called tadpoles. These tadpoles swim about the pond feeding. They grow bigger. Soon they grow two hind legs. Later, they get two front legs. Then they lost their tails. Soon after this, they come out of the water and hop about on the bank. They are now tiny, baby frogs. At last they grow into full-grown frogs. So the first part of the life of a frog is spent in the water. But full-grown frogs live both in water and on land. So they are called by a Latin name amphibian meaning "living in both".

27. The Crow

The crow is a large black bird, with a grey head. It is very common. Everybody knows it. Crows live in villages and towns, for the sake of food they can pick up. They are very noisy birds. Their voices are harsh and loud. The noise they make is called "cawing"; they call out, "caw, caw!'. So the Indian name for a crow is *kawwa*. Crows are bold, cheeky birds. They are clever thieves. They sit round a house watching for a chance of stealing. They swoop down at once on any waste food thrown out. They steal food left on the verandah. They even come right into the house to steal. So house-servants do not like them at all. But crows do some good things. They eat up rubbish and rotting food. This would cause diseases if left about.

28. The Parrot

The parrot is well known for its talking powers. Some kinds of parrots are better at talking than others. But most parrots can talk a little. The best talker is the grey African parrot. It is a large grey bird, with a red tail. These parrots are caught young. Then they can be tamed and trained. They are quick at copying people's voices. They say over the words whatever they hear. Soon they can talk a lot. The best way of teaching them is in the dark. A cloth is put over the cage; or the cage is lowered down at a dark well. Then one can say words over and over again to the parrot. It listens and learns the words. The common Indian green parrot can also be taught to talk. But it does not talk so well as the African parrot. Only tame parrots talk. Wild parrots only scream loudly and harshly.

29. The Pigeon

The pigeon is a very common bird. Some kinds of pigeons are found in almost all countries. In Urdu the pigeon is called *Kabutar*. Pigeons are bred and kept for food, like fowls. They make good eating. The pretty fancy kinds are kept as pets. They are very tame. They will feed out of their master's hands, and sit on his shoulders. In big towns they are not hunted. They are great favourites with the people. Flocks of pigeons fly and walk round St. Paul's Cathedral in London, and the Piazza in Venice. They are quite tame, and the people feed them. Pigeons are strong fliers. One kind is called the "homing-pigeon". It is so called because it can always find its way back home. Homing-pigeons are used to carry messages. The messages are on small bits of paper tied under the pigeon's wings. So they act like postmen.

30. The Peacock

The male peacock is a beautiful bird. Its neck is covered with lovely blue feathers. Its body is green and blue. Its glory is its long tail. It can open its tail like a great fan. The colours are blue and green and gold. The bird is very proud of its tail. It opens it, and struts about to be admired. The peacock stands for pride. We say, "as proud as a peacock". The Female peacock (peahen) is a plain brown bird. She has no tail like the male bird. Peacock has all the beauty. In India peacocks are sacred birds. The peacock is called the mount of Saraswati the goddess of learning. So it is very wrong to kill a peacock. But peacocks are great thieves. They do great damage to growing crops. Some people say that peacocks kill snakes. Some say they can smell the coming rain. Then they give harsh screams.

31. The Ostrich

The Ostrich is the largest of all birds. Some ostriches are eight feet high. The ostrich is so strong that like a horse, it can carry a man. It has a long neck and a small head. It carries its head and neck erect. Its wings are small, and it cannot fly. But it has very strong legs. It can run faster than a horse. it defends itself by kicking. A kick from an ostrich can lame a horse, or kill a man. The ostrich is found in Africa. It lives in dry sandy wastes, or country covered with low bushes. It feeds on grass, leaves, seeds and berries. Wild ostriches are very shy. They are hard to catch, for they run so fast. Ostrich are hunted for the sake of their feathers. Ostrich-feathers are very costly. Ladies in Western Countries buy them for their hats. Ostriches are now bred in large farms in Africa. The sale of their feathers pays well.

32. The Owl

The owl is a very solemn-looking bird. It has big round eyes and a solemn face. It sits quite still for a long time. It seems to be thinking deeply. So some people think it is a very wise bird. With the old Romans, the owl was sacred to Minerva, the goddess of wisdom. But some people think it looks stupid. So they call a person they think foolish an "owl". The owl is a night-bird. All day it sleeps in a dark old tower, or a hole in a tree. It comes out at night to hunt. It can see in the dark. The owl hunts for mice and other small animals, and small birds. It sits in a tree and "hoots". A mouse below in the grass hears the sound. It trembles and moves the grass. The owl above hears the rustle. It swoops softly down, and catches the frightened mouse.

33. Birds of Prey

Most kinds of birds feed on seeds and fruits, insects and worms. But some kinds hunt for small animals and other small birds. These are called 'birds of prey.' They hunt for their prey, like lions and tigers. Eagles, hawks, kites and vultures are birds of prey. They all have sharp curved beaks, and strong claws, and big wings. The eagle is called the king of birds. There are several kinds of eagles. They are rare birds, and live up in the mountains. Some eagles will attack even sheep. The hawk is a smaller bird, but looks like the eagle. Hawks prey on small animals and birds. Men train hawks to hunt for them. Hunting with hawks is called "hawking". The trained hawk is sent up after even such a big bird as a heron. It flies above the heron, attacks it, and brings it down. Vultures are very big birds. They feed on dead bodies.

34. The Bee

Bees make honey. We all like honey. We keep bees in bee-houses made of straw, called "hives". Honey-bees live together in companies, called "swarms". Each swarm must have its own hive. There are three kinds of bees in every swarm. First, there is the queen-bee, the mother of the whole swarm. She does nothing all her life except laying eggs. Then there are the male-bees, called "drones". They laze about and eat honey. But when one has married the queen-bee, all the rest are killed. Most of the bees are workers. They are always working. So we say, "As busy as a bee". In a new hive they first make the wax honey-combs for storing honey. Then some fly out to gather nectar from flowers to make into honey. Some feed the queen-bee, and look after her eggs. Some are always sweeping and cleaning. Some guard the door of the hive.

35. The Ant

There are many kinds of ants. All kinds live in companies, as men live in towns. Most kinds make their ant-towns underground. There they live in the tunnels and rooms they make. Ants are always busy. They work hard all their short lives. So the wise King Solomon said, "Go to the ant, thou sluggard; learn of her ways, and be wise." There are two classes of ants in an ant-town. The soldier-ants form one class. They protect the ant-town, and fight other kinds of ants. The rest are the workers. They feed the young ants, fetch from outside, dig, build, carry loads and clean. They are always doing something. Some large kinds of ants keep slaves. They catch smaller ants and bring them to their ant-town. There they keep them, and make them work. The ant is a very clever kind of insect.

36. The Spider

The name spider means *spinner*. Spiders are insects that spin webs. Some build their webs in trees and bushes. Some build them in rooms. They are the "cobwebs" that hang in the ceiling. The spider's webs is not a house to live in. It is a trap. Spiders feed on flies. They spin their webs to catch flies. So a spider's web is like a fisherman's net. How does a spider make its web? The spider has inside it a kind of gum. It draws this gum out in fine threads. It makes its web, or "fly-net", with these threads. When the web is ready, the spider sits in the middle. It is waiting for a fly. Soon a fly flies into the web. There it sticks. It cannot get away. The spider runs out over the web. It kills the struggling fly. Then it sucks all the juice out of it.

37. The Mosquito

In India we all know mosquitoes too well. How they tease us on hot summer nights! They buzz and sing round our ears. They bite our faces and hands when we are asleep. What a nuisance they are! They are also a danger. How do we get malarial fever? From the bites of mosquitoes. Yes, it is the mosquito that gives people fever. The mosquito puts a kind of poison into our blood. So we must guard ourselves against mosquitoes. We should always sleep under mosquito nets. Then the mosquitoes cannot get at us to bite us. Or we can cover our hands and faces with kerosene oil. Mosquitoes do not like the smell of this oil. They keep away from it. But the best way is to get rid of the mosquitoes. How can this be done? By draining all stagnant pools. For mosquitoes begin their life as tiny grubs in the water.

38. The Butterfly

Butterflies are pretty and harmless insects. They do not work like bees. They are not clever like ants. But their beauty gives us pleasure. Their chief beauty is their wings. They are of bright colours (red, green, blue, yellow, white, black), arranged in pretty patterns. The life-story of a butterfly is strange. The female lays its eggs on the leaf of a plant. After some weeks these eggs hatch out into little worms with legs, called caterpillars. These caterpillars at once begin to feed on the leaf. They live like this for a few weeks. Then each caterpillar makes a covering for itself, called a cocoon. It goes to sleep in this cocoon. There it sleeps all the winter. When the warm weather comes back, it comes out. The caterpillar bursts its cocoon, and comes out a lovely butterfly.

39. The House-Fly

We all know the common fly. In the hot weather flies are a great nuisance. They come into our houses and buzz about. They crawl over our faces and tickle us. They crawl over our food at meal times. We flap them away, and kill a few. But still more come and worry us. Flies are more than troublesome. They are dangerous. They lay their eggs in our meat; and the meat goes bad. Then flies can gives us some diseases. They feed on all kinds of rotten stuff. Then they come and sit on the cakes and fruit and sweets in the bazaar. They leave disease germs on the food we eat. Then we get the diseases. So flies are dirty and dangerous insects. We must cover up our food against them. And we must drive them away or kill them if we can.

40. The Coconut Tree

The coconut palm is a beautiful tree. Its trunk is like a tall slender pillar. At the top is a circle of grand leaves shaped like feathers. It is a very useful tree. Every part of it is used for something. The coconut, its fruit, gives men food and drink. Also from it is got coconut oil, used in making soap and candles. The strong, brown fibre round the nut is made into "coir", used for making mats and ropes. The hard shell of the nut is used as a cup. A pleasant drink is made from the sap or juice of the tree; also a wine called palm-wine. The juice is also made into a kind of very sweet sugar, called "jaggery." The huge leaves are used for making the roofs of houses. They are also woven into mats and baskets. The wood of the trunk is used for building.

41. The Sugar-Cane

The sugar-cane is a tall plant. It has long, thick stems, with long green leaves on the top. The stem or "cane" contains sweet juice. Sugar is made out of this juice. Some canes, cut into lengths, are sold in the bazaar. They are chewed raw and sucked for the sake of the sweet juice. But most of the canes go to the sugar-mills to make sugar. There they are first crushed under heavy rollers. These squeeze out the sweet sap or juice. The juice is then heated in shallow pans. The water all goes off in vapour. The solid sugar is left in the bottom of the pans. Part of this becomes white sugar crystals. Part of it becomes thick brown molasses or treacle. India is the home of the sugar-cane. Yet much of the sugar we eat came, till India became free, from other countries.

42. The Plantain

The plantain, or banana is not a tree. It is a very large plant. It grows to be eighteen feet high. It has long creeping roots under the ground. From these roots rise thick, fleshy stems. The leaves are at the top of the stems. They are very large; sometimes ten feet long. The flowers come out in long purple spikes. They are followed by the fruit—the bananas we buy in the bazaar. Plantains need a lot of water. They grow best in hot, moist climates. So they grow well in Bengal, Madras and Bombay. Bananas are very wholesome fruits. They are a good food. They are generally eaten raw when ripe. But they are very nicely roasted. They are also dried and crushed to powder. The flour thus made is baked into cakes and bread. Bananas are sent in ships to England. They are packed when green, and ripen on the voyage.

43. The Bamboo

The bamboo is a very useful plant. Its long stems are very strong. They are used as props in house-building. They are also used as spears and *lathis*. Bamboo stems are partly hollow. They are divided by solid rings into sections. These sections are cut out, and made into buckets, pipes and cups. Of the thinner stems, chairs, tables, screens and other furniture are made. Bamboo furniture is light and cheap. Bamboo stems are also split into thin strips. These strips are fastened together to make *chicks*. *Chicks* are blinds for windows and doors to keep out flies and the glare of the sun. Horses are fond of the young tender shoots of the bamboo. In many countries these are eaten by people as a vegetable. A coarse kind of paper is made from the bamboo. So the bamboo serves many purposes. Bamboos are found chiefly in India, China, Japan and Africa.

44. Wheat

The chief food of cows, horses, sheep and men is the same. They all eat grass. These animals eat the leaves of grass. We eat the seeds. Wheat is a kind of grass. We grind its seeds into flour. Of wheat flour we make bread. And bread is our chief food. Bread is called "the staff of life". In India, wheat is a *rabi*, or spring crop. The seed is sown in the cold weather. The harvest is reaped in March or April. When the wheat has been reaped, it is threshed. The seeds are beaten out of their husks, or hard coverings. Then the wheat is winnowed. The seeds and dry husks are tossed up in the wind. The wind blows away the light husks, or chaff. The heavy seeds are left behind. The seeds then go to the miller. He grinds them into flour. The baker makes loaves of bread with the flour.

45. Rice

Rice is a kind of grass. It needs a warm, moist climate. It grows well in Bengal, Chennai, Mayanmar and parts of China. So the people of those countries are rice-eaters. Rice grows in water. The rice-fields are closed in with low mounds of earth. They are kept flooded. The young rice plants are planted in the mud under the water. The green leaves rise above the water. The rice-fields look very green. The rice we eat is the seed of the plant. The ripe seeds are covered with a rough brown husk. In this form rice is called Dhan. The white, hard seed with the husk taken off is called chawal, or husked rice. Rice is boiled, and then eaten without curry or dal. It is also a good food.

46. Tobacco

Tobacco-smoking is a common habit now, but this has been said that it is a bad habit. Heavy smoking may do harm. It is very soothing but should be avoided. Tobacco is smoked in pipes, or as cigars and cigarettes smoking is injurious to health. In India it is often smoked in the *hookah*, or waterpipe. The tobacco we smoke is the dried leaf of the tobacco plant. The plant grows in hot countries. It is grown in America and the West Indies, Japan, Indonesia, and India. Tobacco cannot be grown in Europe. It is too cold there. But raw tobacco is taken to England to be manufactured. The green tobacco leaves are at first dried in the sun. Then they are treated with chemicals, and cut by machines. Tobacco was first brought to Europe by Sir Walter Raleigh in Queen Elizabeth's reign, over three hundred years ago.

47. Potato

The potato is an American plant. Sir Walter Raleigh brought it to Europe more than three hundred years ago. He first planted it in Ireland. It became the chief food of the Irish people. Now it is known and eaten all over the world. It is so common that everyone knows it. The potato plant grows low on the ground. It bears pretty white flowers. Its fruit is a small red berry. But it is not the fruit that we eat. The fruit is poisonous. We eat the roots. The roots are round like balls. When properly boiled or roasted they are a wholesome food. Europeans always eat potatoes as a vegetable at their dinners. Potato plants grow best in light, well-drained soil. They are now carefully cultivated. So the potatoes we eat are far bigger and finer than those Sir Walter Raleigh brought home.

48. Tea

Tea is the dried leaves of the tea plant.The tea plant is a low bush. The leaves are gathered from the bushes four times a year. The green leaves are first dried in the sun. Then they are rolled, and roasted in iron pots. Afterwards, they are dried again over charcoal fires. The drink is made in a tea-pot. Dry tea leaves are put into the pot. Boiling water is then poured in, and the pot is covered with a lid. After a few minutes, the tea is ready to drink. English people and Indians take their tea with milk and sugar. The Russians mix lemon juice with it. The Chinese drink it neat. Tea is a soothing and harmless drink. It refreshes us when we are tired. Bit it must not be drunk too often or too much. Then it will do harm to the nerves. Tea is grown in China, Japan, India and Ceylon. It first came from China.

49. Rubber

Rubber is very useful. It is tough, elastic and water-proof. The tyres of motor-cars and bicycles are made of rubber. It is used, also, for making balls, boot-soles, belts, toys, rain-coats, and other things. What is rubber? It is the gum in the bark of certain trees. Rubber-trees grow in hot countries, like Africa. They grow wild in the forests. To get the gum, the bark of the tree is cut. A little cup is tied under this cut. The liquid gum slowly drips into the cup. It is then dried in the sun. It becomes thick and hard. Then it is cleaned and made into India-rubber. Rubber-trees are now grown in plantations. There are many in Malaysia and Indonesia. It pays to grow these trees. For rubber is in great demand now. It fetches a good price in the market.

50. Cotton

The cotton plant needs a warm climate and rich black soil. It is grown in America, Egypt and India. In India cotton is a *kharif*, or autumn crop. It is planted in the rainy season. By October the plants bear their pretty yellow flowers. Then the pods form. They contain soft white fibres round the seeds. From these fibres cotton thread is made. The raw cotton is gathered in November. It is first separated from the seeds and cleaned. This is called "ginning". There are ginning mills to do this work. The cleaned raw cotton goes to the spinning mills. There it is drawn into cotton thread. This cotton thread then goes to the weaving mills. There it is woven into cotton cloth. The seeds of the cotton plant are not thrown away. They contain a very useful oil. The cotton plant is therefore very useful.

51. Silk

Our clothes are made of cotton, or wool, or silk. We get cotton from a plant. We get wool from an animal. We get silk from an insect, the silkworm. Silkworms are the caterpillars of the silkworm-moth. The moth lays its eggs on mulberry leaves. Some months after, the eggs hatch out into caterpillars. These are the silkworms. They feed on the mulberry leaves for about a month. They then spin round them soft yellow coverings, called cocoons. In them they go to sleep. In a few weeks they will wake up and come out as white moths. But to get the silk, men put the cocoons into hot ovens. The heat kills the silkworms. The cocoons are then unwound. They are made of fine, smooth threads. These threads are silk. Men weave them into lovely silk cloth. They keep regular silk-worm farms, planted with mulberry trees.

52. Paper

Paper used to be made from cotton and linen cloth. Paper thus made is called "rag-paper". But most paper is made of the fibres of different plants. Straw, grass and wood are used. Most of the paper we use today is made of wood-pulp. Wood-pulp is wood crushed by machines into a soft wet mass. Whole forests are used up every year to make wood-pulp. This is because such a lot of paper is needed for books and newspapers. Before paper was made, men had to write on animal skins, called parchment. This was before the days of printing. The invention of paper came just in time for printing. We could not have had cheap books without printing. And printing would have been of little use without cheap and easily made paper. In the 19th century English people learnt to make paper by machinery.

53. Gold

Gold is the most precious of all metals. It is so precious because it is so rare. It is found in only a few places in the world. Gold is also the most beautiful of all metals. Its bright yellow colour is very pretty. It takes a fine polish. It is also a soft metal. So it can be easily worked. Gold is used to make ornaments, like rings, bracelets and brooches. The crowns of Kings are made of gold. There used to be gold coins also, like the English sovereign. A sovereign was a small coin, about as big as a fifty-paisa piece. Gold is much more precious than silver. The word "gold" sometimes means money. When we say a man loves gold, we mean money.

54. Iron

Iron is a common and cheap metal. This is a good thing, for iron is the most useful of all metals. Think of the things made of iron and steel! Tools, machines, engines, bridges, ships, cars, railways, and many more. Iron is found in certain kinds of rocks. The iron found mixed with rock is called iron-ore. The iron-ore is first crushed by machines. Then it is melted in very hot furnaces. The iron flows out as a white hot liquid into moulds. There it cools. In that state it is called cast-iron or pig-iron. Cast-iron is brittle. To make it tough, it is again melted and stirred about. Then it is beaten, red-hot, with heavy hammers. It becomes wrought-iron. Wrought-iron is very strong and tough. Out of wrought-iron steel is made. Steel is the most perfect form of iron. It takes a bright polish, and can be ground down to a very fine point or sharp edge.

55. Coal

Coal is used chiefly as fuel. It makes good, hot fires. It keeps our houses warm in the cold weather. It is used for cooking. It is burnt in engines to make steam. But coal has also other uses. Coal gas, for lighting, comes from it. Coal-tar is useful in many ways. Tar is used as paint. Tar keeps wood from rotting. Dyes for colouring cloth are obtained from coal-tar; also scents and some medicines. So coal is very useful. Coal is found deep under the ground. Deep mines have to be sunk to take it out. Miners go down these mines and dig the coal out of the rock. Coal is really very, very old wood. That is why it burns so well. It is the wood of forests that grew ages ago. They have been pressed under masses of rock for ages. Time and pressure turned the wood into a sort of stone.

56. Salt

Salt is very useful. Indeed, we could not live without it. First, it gives flavour to food. Meat, bread and vegetables would be tasteless without salt. Salt is really necessary for meat-eaters. Meat cooked without salt makes them unhealthy. Then salt keeps things from going bad. Fish or meat kept in salt will keep good for a long time. Salt is found in two forms. There is liquid salt and solid salt. Sea-water is full of salt. In some places there are brine-springs. They flow out of the rocks like fresh springs. Salt is also found in the form of rock. This is called rock-salt. It is dug up out of the ground. There are salt mines in the Salt Range of hills in Punjab. Salt is got out of the sea in this way. Sea-water is put into shallow pools. The water dries up. The white salt crystals are left at the bottom.

57. Water

Water has many uses. In fact we could not live without it. If a man is kept without water, he dies. So the first use of water is for drinking. Not only that.

We could get no food without water. Plants must have water. Without water we could not have vegetables, fruit or bread. And we should not have any meat. For animals must have grass to eat, and grass must have water. So water is needed by all living things. No water, no life. Then we need water for keeping clean. We wash our bodies, clothes, rooms and everything, with water. We must keep clean to keep healthy. Water, too, is power. Men use moving water to work mills and machines. Water-power (like running streams and waterfalls) is much cheaper than steam. And steam itself is simply water in another shape. No water, no steam-engines.

58. Milk

Cow milk is the most popular drink forever. Buffalo's milk is very rich. Goat's milk is rather bitter. In some lands men drink the milk of camels. But cow's milk is the best. Milk is a perfect food. Babies and young children live on it. It is the best kind of food for sick people. Milk is taken in tea. It is used for making many kinds of puddings. There are egg-pudding, custard, *firni* and others. Milk can be turned into curd by certain acids. Curd is eaten largely in India. In England it is called junket. From the cream of milk, butter is made. Butter is eaten with bread. In India, *ghee,* which is melted butter, is used in most dishes. Cheese also is made from milk. Cheese is a wholesome food.

59. Dress

Animals and birds grow their own clothes. Sheep are covered with wool, bears with fur, dogs with hair, and birds with feathers. But men have to make their own clothes. Dress is worn for three reasons. It is worn for warmth, for decency, for show. In cold countries clothes are needed to keep us warm. In hot countries clothes are not needed. But even in hot lands, most people wear clothes for the sake of decency. Then much dress is worn for ornament. Some people like to wear grand clothes. They do so to make themselves look better. Fine clothes do not make a gentleman. It is foolish to spend too much on fine clothes. It is a form of vanity. But a gentleman will always see that his dress is neat and clean.

60. An Umbrella

The word umbrella means "little shade". So the name tells us what the thing is for. An umbrella is a shade from the sun or a shelter from the rain. It is fixed on a stick with a handle. It can open and shut. In the rain, we open it and hold it over our heads. Or we can carry it rolled up like a stick when we do not need it. So an umbrella is very handy and useful. In Kolkata, every Bengali carries an umbrella as a shade from the hot sun. During rains in England people carry umbrellas lest they should get wet. Now-a-days people keep umbrellas for use. But in old days the umbrella was a sign of rank. In Burma, only the king and great lords were allowed umbrellas.

61. The Clock

The clock is for measuring time. It tells us, at any moment, the time of day. In old days men had to watch the sun and the moon to know the time. Then they made the sun-dial. But this told the time only when the sun was shining. The English King, Alfred, measured time by burning marked candles. Another plan was the sand-glass or the hour-glass. But clocks and watches are the best time-measures. A clock is a wonderful machine. A wound-up spring moves a number of wheels. They move the clock-hands round the dial or face of the clock. The round face is marked with figures for the twelve hours. There are also marks for the sixty minutes in each hour. When we want to know the time, we look at the clock. The small hand points after XII. The big hand points to VI. We know it is half-past-twelve o'clock.

62. The Swimming

Most animals can swim right off the first time they go into the water. But men have to learn. Someone who knows how to swim has to teach us. Everybody should learn to swim. Why? First, it is a very good exercise. Doctors say it is the best exercise. In swimming all the muscles of the body are used. Secondly, swimming gives great pleasure. How nice it is to have a swim on a hot, dusty summer day? Thirdly, knowing how to swim may one day save one's life. We never know when we may be in danger from the water. Your ship may be wrecked on a voyage. The pleasure-boat you are in may upset. You may slip off the bank into a river. If you cannot swim, you may be drowned. But swimming may save your life. Lastly, by swimming you may one day save another's life.

63. The Sun

We could not live at all without the sun. The sun gives us light and heat and life. Suppose the sun went out, like a crackle ! What would happen ? It would be always night. We should be in complete darkness. Next, it would be very, very cold. The earth would be all snow and ice. Then all plants and animals and men would die. There would be no life. This would be a cold, dark, dead world. Yet we could not bear the sun all the time. The earth would become too hot to live in. We need the night to bring us rest and sleep. We get night and day because our earth is always spinning round like a top. So one side of the earth sees the sun, and it is day. The other side is hidden from the sun, and there it is night. The earth takes twenty-four hours to spin right round.

64. The Moon

The moon is a round ball, like the earth. But it is much smaller than the earth. The moon goes round the earth. It takes about twenty-eight days to go around the earth. So we call twenty-eight days a month; that is, a "moonth". The moon is the natural satellite of earths. The light given by the moon is not its own light. It is not a mass of fire like the sun. It is a cold, dead mass of rock. Its light comes from the sun shining on it. So moonlight is really second-hand sunlight. It borrows its light from the sun. So moonlight is soft and dim, as compared with sunshine. During each month the moon seems to change its shape. But it does not really change. All the time it is a round ball. But we can see only that part of it which is lit up by the sun. The rest is dark.

65. The Earth

In old times men thought the earth was flat. Now we know it is a round ball. It is a very big ball. It is 25,000 miles round. But it does not stand still. It floats in space. All the time it is rushing through space very fast. It moves in a circle round the sun. It takes a year to go right round the sun. At the same time it is turning round on itself. It spins round like a top. It takes twenty-four hours to spin right round. It is this spinning of the earth that makes day and night. When our part of the earth sees the sun, it is day with us. When it is turned away from the sun, it is night. To us the sun seems to be going round the earth. But this is because we are spinning round with the earth. The sun does not move.

66. The Sea

Look at a map of the world. You will see how much of its surface is sea. Three quarters of the earth is covered by water. But this vast mass of water is not wasted. The sea does much to make life on earth possible. First, the sea gives us rain. The south-west trade-wind comes to India after crossing over thousands of miles of sea. On its way it takes up a lot of water-vapour from the sea. This turns into rain when it is cooled by the Ghats. Then the monsoon breaks. The rainy season begins. Secondly, the sea supplies us with fresh air. The winds blowing in from the sea are fresh and health-giving. Thirdly, the sea gives us a lot of wholesome food. It is full of fish. Fishermen catch the fish for our food. It also gives us salt. Lastly, men use the sea as a road. They travel to distant lands by sea in their ships.

67. Rivers and their Uses

A river is a great drain. In towns men make drains to carry away the rain-water. These drains keep the town from being flooded. So the first use of a river is to carry surplus rain-water off the land to the sea. Rivers also carry sand and mud down from the mountains to the plains. This makes fertile land. The Gangetic Plain in India has been made by the Ganges. The river Nile has made the land of Egypt. In dry countries rivers feed irrigation canals. In Punjab the water of its Five Rivers has made millions of acres of land fertile by canals. Rivers, too, are roads. They are waterways for boats and ships. People can travel by river. Much merchandise is carried for hundreds of miles by river-boats. So rivers are useful in many ways. Besides some rivers, are very beautiful.

68. Mountains and their Uses

Mountains help men in three ways. They give us fresh air, fresh water and fresh soil. First, mountains keep the air moving and so fresh. Hot air rises; cold air falls. The hot air of the plains rises to the mountains. The snow-covered mountains cool it. It comes down again to the plains as fresh cool winds. Secondly, mountains attract and catch rain and snow. The rain sinks down into under-ground caves. These are the sources of the streams and rivers, which flow down to the plains. The rivers are fed also by the snow melting on the mountains in the summer. Lastly, the rocks on the mountains are split up by the frost. Broken pieces are washed down by the rivers. The rivers grind them down into sand and earth. They lay this on the land below, when in flood. In this way the land is enriched.

69. Clouds

What are clouds? How do they give rain? Well, sun-warmed air sucks up water from the sea as vapour. You cannot see vapour but it is there. Warm air can hold a lot of this unseen vapour. Warm air rises. This warm air, full of water-vapour, rises high up in the sky. There the air is cold. The rising warm air gets chilled. Cold air cannot hold so much vapour. Some of the vapour condenses. That is, it turns back into tiny drops of water. It can now be seen as mist or cloud. Winds carry the cloud into still colder air. The tiny drops run together and make big drops. These big drops of water are too heavy to float in the air. They fall to the earth below, and we say, "It is raining." This is how the rain comes. So clouds are a great blessing. They give us rain.

70. Monsoon

The rainy season in India is due to the monsoon. The monsoon is the wind that blows from the south-west from June to September. In the old days of the sailing ships, traders used to depend on this wind. It blew their ships from south-west to India. So the wind was called the "trade-wind". In October or November the wind changes its direction, and blows from the north-east. It carries the traders' ships back again. The monsoon, or south-west trade-wind, comes to India over the Indian Ocean. It blows over thousands of miles of sea. So it reaches India full of moisture or water-vapour. It strikes against the Western Ghats, and is cooled by the cold rocks. It can no longer hold all its water-vapour. This condenses and falls as rain. The rainy season then begins. The dried up grass revives. The farmers begin ploughing. The thirsty land rejoices.

71. A Thunderstorm

There are black clouds away in the south-west. The air is very still. Everything seems to be waiting. The dark arch of cloud is coming nearer. There is a rumble of far-off thunder. There, a flash of lightning. A cool wind begins to blow. It smells of rain. The thunder sounds nearer and louder. The lightning is brighter. Now the sky above is dark with clouds. The wind becomes a gale, roaring past. A blinding lightning flash ! A fearful crash of thunder ! The rain pours down like a water-fall. For half-an-hour the storm rages. The thunder crashes and rolls. The lightning flashes. The wind blows with fury. The rain pelts down. Then the storm passes. The blue sky is seen. The rain stops. The wind dies down. The sun shines out. The air is cool and clean. The earth is wet and soft. The streams are full of rushing water. Grass and trees are fresh and green.

72. The Rainbow

A rainbow is a beautiful sight. It is a perfect arch of coloured light in the sky. We see it only when it is raining and the sun is shining at the same time. What makes a rainbow? Well, white sunlight is really made up of seven colours. They are—violet, indigo, blue, green, yellow, orange and red. A ray of light, passed through a prism (a three-sided piece of glass), is split into these seven colours. The falling drops of rain act like little prisms. They split up the white sunlight into its seven colours. We see them in the rainbow. It is a *bow*, or arch, made by the *rain*. That is why there must be rain and sunshine at the same time to get a rainbow. When the rain stops, or the sun disappears, the rainbow fades away. A rainbow is taken as a sign of hope.

73. Echoes

Sometimes a boy at play throws a ball against a wall. The ball hits the wall and bounces back. The boy catches it in his hands. An echo is like that. In some places there are echoes. We shout against a tall rock or the side of a house. We hear our shout repeated. The sound comes back to us. This is an echo. Some echoes are very clear and good. They repeat words and whole sentences. We shout, "Who are you?" The echo answers quite clearly, "Who are you?" Our question bounces back from the rock into our ears. Sounds do not travel very fast. So it takes a little time for our voice to reach the rock and come back to us. This is why we hear our words repeated after we have said them. They have to go and come back, like the boy's ball.

74. Deserts

There are parts of the world that get no rain. They are great wastes of dry sand and rock. The sun beats down on them all day. They are very hot. These places are called deserts. Some, like the Arabian Desert and the Sahara, are hundreds of miles across. Travelling over deserts is difficult and dangerous. There are no roads. Carts and motor-cars would sink in the sand. The only way is to ride on a camel. The camel is called "the ship of the desert". It is the only animal that can make a long journey across a desert. It is dangerous for a man to travel alone. Men go in companies, called caravans. They all ride on camels. They carry plenty of food and drink with them. There are places in a desert with springs of water. They are called "oases". A caravan travels from oasis to oasis.

75. Fresh Air

We cannot live without air. No air means death at once. Bad air means bad health. We must have fresh air to keep well and strong. A crowded, stuffy room soon gives one a headache. Why is this? It is because we are breathing bad air. The air we breathe out is full of a poisonous gas. In the open air this gas is blown away by the wind. But in a closed room it cannot get away. We breathe it in again and again. This makes us feel sleepy. It gives us a headache. When we move out again into the fresh air, we feel all right. But people living long in bad air get really ill. Their lungs get diseased, and they may die. We need fresh air to purify our blood and give it more life. So we should be out-of-doors as much as we can. In a room, we must keep the windows open.

76. Well Begun is Half Done

A good start gives a great advantage. For example, a football team scores a goal in the first half. It is greatly encouraged. The opposing team is just as much discouraged. The first goal may mean the winning of the match. This is also true in war. The first battle counts for much. A victory at the very beginning gives an army a great advantage. The enemy, also, are disheartened from the first. As another proverb says, "It is the first step that counts". But the proverb does not say that well begun is *all* done—but only *half* done. We may begin well, and yet end badly. The first step certainly counts, and counts a lot. But without second and third and fourth steps we shall get nowhere. We must not only *begin* well; we must also *go on* well. Then we shall have a chance of finishing well.

77. Habits

Habits, good and bad, are all formed in the same way. They are formed by repetition. We do something in a special way. We do it again in the same way. We do it more and more in that way. At last it becomes a habit to do it in that way. It is like people making a footpath by always treading the earth down in one direction. Our habits are important. They form our characters. Character is just a bundle of habits. Repeated acts form habits; habits make up character; character decides one's success or failure in life. "Sow the thought, and reap the act. Sow the act, and reap the habit. Sow the habit, and reap the character. Sow the character, and reap your fate." Habits can be good or bad. Good habits form a good character. Bad habits form a bad character. So we must try to form only good habits.

78. Do it Now

"Punctuality" is a long word. It means doing things at the right time. A punctual boy is never late for school. He has his home-work done at the right time. He does not keep his family waiting at meal-time. Punctuality is a habit. We can get into the way of doing things at the right time. But it is not easy at first. It is easier to dawdle and laze about. It is so easy to put things off. We say, "We will do it tomorrow, or next week." So we get into the bad habit of being late for everything. Once we get into this bad habit, it is hard to get out of it. A good motto to keep before one is, "Do it *now*!" An unpunctual person is one's own enemy. And such a person is a nuisance to everyone else. An unpunctual clerk soon loses his job. A friend who always keeps us waiting may lose our friendship.

79. Hobbies

A hobby is an amusement. It is anything we like doing that is not our regular work. What is a business to one, may be a hobby to another. For example, gardening is a paid gardener's work; but to a clerk, gardening may be a hobby. There are many kinds of hobbies. Many make collecting things a hobby. Some collect foreign stamps; some collect coins; others collect pictures or books. Other hobbies are games, such as golf, tennis, cricket, chess, cards. Others are some form of sport, such as hunting, fishing, or boating. Photography is an interesting hobby. So is gardening. It is a good thing to have a hobby of some sort. A hobby will keep a boy amused in his holidays. It may also keep him out of mischief. Our hobby, will also give us something to do in old age. It is something to fall back upon when our working days are over.

80. A Stitch in Time Saves Nine

You find a small hole in your coat. You say, "It is only a little one; I will mend it later." It gets bigger and bigger. At last you try to mend it. It now takes a lot of time and trouble to do so. At first one stitch would have done it. Now it takes nine stitches to mend it. So learn the motto, "Do it now". Take things in time. Put things right at once before they go very wrong. Correct faults when they are small. Check a bad habit at the very beginning. Even a kingdom may be lost by neglecting a horse-shoe nail. "For want of a nail, the shoe was lost, for want of a shoe, the horse was lost; for want of a horse, the rider was lost; for want of the rider, the battle was lost; for want of the battle, the kingdom was lost."

81. Thrift

Thrift means the wise care of money. A thrifty man spends his money wisely, and saves all he can. The words "thrift" and "thrive" are connected. To thrive means to be successful and prosperous. Thrift makes a man thrive. Careless people waste their money. They save nothing and run into debt. And debt leads to much unhappiness. How can we be thrifty? We must have some method in using our money. We should plan out what we can do with our month's pay. First, we should buy the things we must have. We need food, fuel, shelter, clothes. Let us make sure of such things first. Next, we should put aside something each month for savings. Only after that should money be spent on pleasures. If we have no money for these, we should go without them. In this way we shall be thrifty people. This is the way to thrive.

82. Discipline

The word discipline comes from the word "disciple". A disciple is a learner. Discipline means learning to obey rules. A child needs discipline. It has first to learn to obey its parents. They know what is best for it. It has to be trained to behave. It is trained by teaching, example and punishment. There must be discipline in a school. School boys and girls have to learn to obey the school rules. They will learn nothing without discipline. Even in games there must be discipline. A football team must obey its captain and the rules of the game. There must be strict discipline in an army. If the soldiers do as they like and will not obey orders they will lose the battle. Above all we must learn self-discipline.

We must learn how to govern ourselves. We must control our tempers and our selfish desires. We must make ourselves do what is right.

83. Slow and Steady Wins the Race

There were two boys in a school. Farid was a clever boy. He answered questions smartly in class. He was quick at sums. Everything seemed to come easy to him. He never seemed to work much. He spent much time in games and fun. Abdul was not clever. Indeed, he was thought dull. He was slow in his work. But he was a hard worker. He plodded steadily at his lessons day by day. In the school examination everyone thought Farid would win the first prize. But everyone was wrong. Farid came in third. It was the plodding Abdul who got the prize. "Slow and steady" won the race. Abdul was the tortoise. Farid was the hare. The hare was so sure of winning that he did not bother to run. The tortoise plodded steadily on and beat the hare in the end. Steady work pays the best.

84. Work

We sometimes envy rich people. They have no work to do. Their life is one long holiday. They must be very happy. But we have to work. Everyday we go to the shop, or the office, or the mill, or the fields. We must work to earn a living. We think we hate work. But we make a mistake. Idleness is not real happiness. No one can be really happy who does nothing all day. Take away our regular daily work, and we should soon be unhappy. Regular work gives us happiness. It is the man who works that can enjoy a holiday. Then work gives us self-respect. It makes us independent. The honest worker can hold his head up. "He looks the whole world in the face, for he owes not any man". Regular work, also, builds up character. It teaches a man good habits. It teaches punctuality, carefulness, thoroughness, perseverance, patience. So work is a blessing.

85. Play

Work is more important than play. But we can not be working all the time. As the old rhyme say:-

"All work and no play
Makes Jack a dull boy".

It is right to play sometimes. So long as play is healthy, it is a good thing. It helps us to work better. Little children play with toys. Older boys and girls play games. Outdoor games are the best. They give us fresh air as well as exercise. Boys and girls both play such games as cricket, football, hockey and tennis. They need skill as well as strength. And they teach us the sporting spirit. They teach us to play together; to play fair; and to lose cheerfully. Then there are indoor games, for wet days. We can then play draughts or chess or different card-games. But we should not mix up play with work. When you play, play; when you work, work.

86. Waste not, Want not

Waste of any kind leads to want. A bad house-keeper wastes food. She buys more than is needed. Some of it goes bad. Some is thrown away. If this goes on long, there will be no more money to buy food. The family will be in want. Some people waste their money. A man has a small income. When he gets his month's pay, he spends much of it on unnecessary things. Before the end of the month he has none left. He must borrow, or the family will starve. If this goes on, he will come to poverty. Many people waste time. A boy is going in for an examination. He wastes a lot of time in idleness and pleasure. He begins to study very late. He has not time enough to prepare. He fails in the examination. So the proverb says, "Waste not, want not". That is, do not waste (anything), and you will not be in want.

87. Presence of Mind

"Presence of mind" means keeping cool in a sudden danger. It is opposite of "losing one's head". In these phrases, both "mind" and "head" mean reason. It is reason that should control our feelings. When we "lose our head" in an accident, our feelings of fright carry us away to do and say silly things. But a man who "keeps his head", or has "presence of mind", still controls his nerves and feelings by his reason. His mind (reason) is still present. Presence of mind is, to some extent, a gift. That is, some people have it naturally. But we can train ourselves to keep our heads.We must practise controlling our feelings. We must learn to check our fears. We can form a habit of self-control. Then we shall be able to keep cool and calm in face of danger.

88. Kind Words

Words have a lot of power. They can help or hurt, bless or curse. Unkind words do a lot of harm. Kind words do a lot of good. We can spoil a friend's happiness by an unkind word. We can cheer up a sad heart with a kind word. And kind words cost nothing. It costs nothing to say a kind word to one who is sad or in trouble. But often a kind word is more welcome than a costly present. So let us try to smile, to speak a cheering word, to say kind things, and so make others happy. Kind words come out of a kind heart. Selfish people think only of themselves. They find it hard to say kind things. But kind hearted people forget themselves. They think of others. So they naturally say kind words. A children's hymn says, "Kind words can never die." It is true. They are not forgotten.

89. All is not Gold that Glitters

Gold is the most precious metal. With its shining yellow colour it is also the most beautiful. It glitters brightly in the light. But other common metals can glitter like gold. Polished brass shines like gold. Base metals can be plated with gold, and they look just like it. Common iron can be gilded; that is painted to look like gold. So "all that glitters is not gold". Things are not what they seem. We can easily be taken in by appearances. We meet a stranger. He has a kind, honest face. He speaks politely. He talks piously. We think, "what a good man !" But later we find that he is a rascal. He seemed to be gold. He was only base metal gilded. He was a "hypocrite"; that is, an *actor*. He acted a part. He pretended to be good. But he was not what he seemed. He "glittered"; but he was not gold.

90. How to be Happy

Happiness is a shy bird. Hunt it, and it will fly away. It is better to set a trap for it, and look the other way. We often find happiness when we are thinking of something else. Pleasure-seekers miss it. Money will not bring it. The rich are not always happy. But there are some things that make for happiness. First, good health. To be happy, obey the laws of health and keep well. Second, work. An idler is rarely a happy man. Workers are generally cheerful. Third, healthy amusements and hobbies for our leisure hours. Games, sports, music and books help to make us happy. Fourth, friendship and pleasant companions. But the true source of happiness lies within. The secret of happiness lies in kindness to others, humility, a clean mind, a clear conscience and an upright life.

91. Moral Courage

There are two kinds of courage. There is physical courage and moral courage. Physical courage is courage to face danger to the body—pain, wounds or death. Moral courage is courage to face jeers, disapproval, unpopula-rity or hatred, for what is right. A man can have one kind of courage without the other. A soldier may be brave in battle, and yet afraid of being laughed at by his mates. He is a moral coward. Another dares to defy public opinion for conscience' sake, and yet is afraid of torture. He is a physical coward. It often takes a lot of moral courage to tell the truth. A schoolboy breaks the rules. He is hauled up before the headmaster. He is afraid of punishment. He tells a lie to shield himself. He is a moral coward. If he had courage he would tell the truth. It takes much moral courage to stand alone and go against public opinion.

92. Union is Strength

You remember the old tale about the bundle of sticks. The old man's sons could not break the sticks tied up in a bundle. But they broke each stick by itself quite easily. In this way he taught them to be a united family. If they worked together as brothers, they would be strong. If they quarrelled and fought, they would be weak. His lesson was, "Union is strength". To be strong, a football team must learn team-work. They must work together as one team. If each member plays his own game, they will lose the match. To win a battle, an army must work as one man. Napoleon's motto was, "Divide and conquer". He tried to split up the allies fighting against him. Then he would attack them one by one. Divided they were weak. A united nation, a united family, a united team, is strong. "United, we stand; divided, we fall."

93. Books and Reading

Suppose someone gave us the key of a treasure house. And suppose he told us, we could go in and take what we liked. Would we not go? Of course we would. We would fill our pockets with gold. Well, a wise man called books "Kings' Treasuries". Kings keep gold and silver and jewels in their treasuries. Books contain something more precious than gold. They contain the riches of knowledge and wisdom. Kings keep their treasuries carefully locked up. They keep the keys themselves. But anyone can have the key to the treasuries of wisdom and knowledge. The key that opens books is just reading. Anyone who can read can open the door and go in and take what he likes. Yet boys at school think learning to read is a great boredom. And when they can read, very few read a book for the love of it. Those who do not read miss much.

94. Rome was not built in a day

The building of a great city like Rome was a long job. It took many days, many years, to build it. And it was not an easy job. It meant hard work and great expense. This is what this proverb means. It is the same with anything worth doing. You have some task to do. You think it will be easy. You soon find it is hard and will take you a long time. You must check your impatience — "Rome was not built in a day". That is, "Be patient". Or you try hard, but you fail again and again. You get discouraged. You feel you must give up trying. Then this word, "Rome was not built in a day", comes as a word of cheer. It says, "Try again, you will succeed."

95. Anger

Anger is not always wrong. Sometimes it is right to be angry. There is holy anger, or righteous indignation. The Bible speaks of "the wrath of God". When is it right to be angry? When we see little children or dumb animals cruelly treated. When the rich oppress the poor. When the strong are unjust to the weak. These things should make us angry. Anger should drive us to help the suffering and protect the helpless. This kind of anger is always unselfish. We are not angry at wrongs done to us. We are angry at wrongs done to others. Such anger springs from love, not from selfishness. But selfish anger is wrong. To be angry with a man for hurting or hating you is wrong. It is wrong because it is selfish. The Bible says, "Love your enemies". Anger leads to hatred. And hatred may lead to massacre.

96. Self-Denial

We spell the first personal pronoun with a capital letter. We write *you, he, she, they,* with small, beginning letters. But *I* is always a capital — a big capital "I". This is natural. For each person thinks more of himself than of anyone else. This means that selfishness is natural to most of us. A child is naturally selfish. His constant cry is, "*I* want this", "*I* will do that"; "*I* won't do what *I* don't like". And many older people are the same. All the time it is "I", "I", "I". Unselfishness has to be learnt. And it is not easy to learn it. Self-denial means denying oneself; denying one's own wishes and will. It is saying "No!" to oneself. It is easy to say "No!" to others. It takes training and effort to learn to say "No!" to oneself. It is hard to write the first personal pronoun with a little "i".

97. Perseverance

"Perseverance" is a long word. It means keeping on till one succeeds. It is sticking to a piece of work till it is finished. It is holding on to the end. Perseverance is necessary to success in anything. The proverb, "Well begun is half done", is only half the truth. It is good to begin well. But that is not enough. We must go on well until we finish. It is easy to begin a piece of work. It is not easy to stick to it till it is done. The Bible says, "He that endures to the end, shall be saved." A boy begins to work for an examination. His subjects are new. At first he finds them easy, and he works well. But after a bit he loses interest, or gets discouraged. At last he gives up regular work. He goes up for the examination. But, of course, he fails.

98. A Rolling Stone Gathers no Moss

You see a stone covered with moss. You know at once it must have been there for years. A stone that is moved about cannot gather moss. Gathering of moss takes time. What does this proverb mean? The "rolling stone" means a fickle, changeable person. A man who never settles down to anything long is a "rolling stone". The proverb says that such a man gains little in life. To get on in business, a man must choose a trade and stick to it. He will never succeed if he keeps changing his trade. To rise to a higher post in his line he must stick to his job. To become a scholar, you must specialize in one subject. It is of no use to chop and change from one subject to another. If you do, you will be "Jack of all trades and master of none." He who hunts two hares loses both.

99. Bad Temper

Anger may sometimes be right and holy. Bad temper is always wrong. It is generally foolish, too. Bad temper is always selfish. Let a selfish person have his own way, and he will be very nice to you. But cross him in the smallest thing, and he flies into a rage. Bad temper is due to lack of self-control. Even the best men feel vexed and cross sometimes. But they control their feelings. They do not lose their temper. But bad-tempered people are the slaves of their feelings. They cannot control feelings. A bad-tempered man is an unhappy man. How can you be happy when every little thing makes you angry? And bad-tempered people make everybody around them unhappy. Bad temper grows into a habit, if not checked. The cure for bad temper is to think less of oneself, and more of others. Learn to control yourself. "When angry, count twelve before you speak."

100. Man's Use of the Forces of Nature

Some of the forces of Nature used by man are wind, water, fire, steam and electricity. Men have caught and tamed these forces for their own use. They have made them serve them like servants. They made the wind grind their corn and drive their ships. They made running water drive their mills. They trained fire to cook their food, warm their houses and smelt iron and other metals. They used steam to drive their railway trains and turn machines in their factories. They caught and tamed even the lightning. Electricity has helped men light their houses and streets; send messages by telegraph and talk to each other at a distance by telephone. And now by wireless we can hear music played a thousand miles away. Men have also tamed animals, such as the horse and the dog, to be their servants.

101. Where there's a Will there's a Way

You want to do a certain thing. But it is hard. You do not know how it can be done. You try one way, but you fail. You try another way, but it is of no use. You think you must give it up. But you *want* to do it very much. You feel you *must* do it, somehow. You think and think. At last you find out how to do it. You have found the way. You try again. You at last succeed. You see, you had the *will* to do it. And you found at last that there was a way to do it. A mere wish or desire is not enough. There must be will and determination. Often we fail because our wish to succeed is not strong enough. It is like a thin, feeble stream of water. It must be strong, rushing torrent, that makes a way for itself.

102. Dirt and Disease

Many diseases are caused by germs. What are germs? They are tiny living creatures. They are so small we cannot see them. They live in water, on land and in the air. One kind gives people cholera, another plague, another small-pox; and so on. We may breathe them in the air. We may drink them in our water. We may eat them in our food. We may catch them from sick people. Now these bad germs love dirt and darkness. They breed in rotten stuff. And they breed very fast. Dirt left in dark corners will breed millions in an hour. If they get into people's food or drink, they will give them disease. Dirt is the mother of disease. Cleanliness is the foe of disease. To avoid these dirt-bred diseases, we must get rid of the dirt. We must keep clean — clean in clothes and person, in houses and streets, in villages and towns.

103. Curiosity

Curiosity simply means a wish to know. So there is nothing wrong in curiosity itself. It all depends on what we are curious about. All children are full of curiosity. They are always asking questions. A child asks, What? Why? How? When? Where? A child's curiosity is a good thing. It is the way it learns. We should always try to answer its questions. Then there is a noble curiosity. It is the curiosity of wise and clever men. They wonder at the things God has made. They want to know all about those things. They search and look and ask questions. All the discoveries of science are due to men's curiosity. Curiosity led James Watt to make the steam-engine. Curiosity led Columbus to discover America. But much curiosity is silly. Some of it is wrong. In small villages people are curious about all their neighbours do. This curiosity leads to gossip; and gossip often does harm.

104. Nothing Venture, Nothing Have

Some people take "Safety first" as their motto. In some ways it is a good motto. It teaches caution, prudence and carefulness. But after all *safety* is the most important thing in life. It is a mistake to put it *first*. Honour, truth, unselfishness are more important than safety. The cautious, timid man says, "Look before you leap". But the bold, adventurous man says, "Nothing venture, nothing have". This means we can gain nothing without taking risks. Columbus would never have discovered America with the motto "Safety first". Prophets like Buddha,

Jesus Christ and Muhammad did not put safety first. They faced persecution and loss for what they believed to be the truth. The timid, overcautions people will get little out of life. The daring and adventurous will get much. Their motto is, "Nothing venture, nothing have".

105. Honesty

Honesty is truthfulness in word and deed. An honest man tells the truth. He says just what he thinks. He will not tell a lie. He does not pretend to feel what he does not feel. He always keeps his promises. You can always trust him. He not only speaks the truth, but also acts truly. As a servant, he does his work honestly and well. As a master, he pays just wages and treats his servants fairly. As a shopkeeper, he sells good stuff at the right price. As a businessman, he deals straight and pays his debts. He will never cheat or steal. An honest man has clear conscience. He can look all men in the face. He owes no man anything. An honest man wins the trust and respect of others. "Honesty is the best policy." An honest man is honest because it is wrong to be dishonest, not because it pays to be honest.

106. Good Manners

Good manners do not come naturally. They have to be learnt. Children have to be taught to behave politely. Without training, they would grow up rough and rude like savages. Good manners are the mark of a gentleman. A real gentleman always tries to consider other people's feelings. He will not say things that will hurt them. He will not speak in a rude way to offend them. He will not do things he knows they do not like. His good manners always show consideration for the feelings of others. That is, he thinks of others, not of himself. So good manners are unselfish manners. A selfish man may be outwardly polite. But he cannot have the spirit of good manners. He always wants his own way. He always seeks his own comfort. A true gentleman thinks of the comfort and happiness of others. He considers their feelings first.

107. No Pains, No Gains

What does taking pains over a thing mean? It means taking trouble over it; doing it with care. The proverb means we cannot gain or achieve anything without care, trouble and hard work. A student wants to become a learned scholar.

Well, "there is no royal road to learning". He will have to study hard and stick to his books. No idler ever won fame as a scholar. A man wants to succeed in business. He will have to work hard. He must be up early, work long hours and take few holidays. "No pains, no gains", is certainly true of business. It is true, also, of character building. Few men are naturally good. A fine, noble character is, as a rule, the result of effort and struggle. One has to take pains to form good habits, to break off bad habits, to resist temptation, to grow virtuous. No one becomes good in his sleep.

108. Cleanliness

Cleanliness is the habit of keeping clean. It is necessary to health. Dirt is the mother of disease. A person who does not wash himself and his clothes will suffer in health. Dirty skin, dirty clothes, dirty houses, dirty villages are all bad for health. To keep well you must keep yourself, your clothes and your house clean. Cleanliness is necessary also to self-respect. A man with dirty clothes, hands and face cannot feel very proud of himself. Certainly others will not respect him. We cannot hope to have decent friends if we do not keep clean. So much for cleanliness of the body. But there is also cleanliness of mind and soul. Sin is dirt. Goodness is cleanliness. We must be clean within as well as without. The Prophet prayed, "*Cleanse* Thou me from secret faults"; "Create in me a *clean heart,* O God!"; "*Wash me*, and I shall be whiter than snow".

109. Exercise

Physical exercise is necessary for health. Physical exercise means exercise of the body. Some get all they need in their daily work. Ploughmen, coolies and blacksmiths work hard with their muscles all day. But clerks, teachers and students do not. They sit all day, working with their heads. They must get some bodily exercise when work is over. Without exercise of some kind they will get weak and fat. Exercise can be taken in many ways. One of the best ways is to play some outdoor game. Football, hockey, cricket, tennis are all good forms of exercise. Riding is a good exercise for those who can afford a horse. Walking suits many people, and it is cheap. Perhaps swimming is the best. It exercises all the muscles of the body. Besides these, there are gymnastics and physical drill. They strengthen the muscles. They improve the general health.

110. Conversation

Good conversation is an art. It is an art worth learning. How can we learn to talk well ? First, remember it takes at least two people to make a conversation. This means that one must be a good listener as well as a good talker. A man who talks all the time spoils conversation. Learn to listen well as well as to talk well. Then learn to talk on subjects that interest others. If you can talk only about things that interest you, you will become a bore. Try to think of things that will interest the other person. Do not be afraid of saying what you really think. But always hear the other side. And do not rudely contradict what others say. In a word, the secret of good conversation is the same as the secret of good manners. It is consideration for the feelings of others.

111. Obedience

Obedience is the habit of doing what we are told to do. It is not easy to learn obedience. But it is necessary. Children must obey their parents. Pupils must obey their teachers. Servants must obey their masters. Soldiers must obey their officers. Subjects must obey the Government. And all men must obey God. Whey should children obey their parents? Because they are ignorant and need training. Why should a servant obey his master? Because he is paid to do what his master wants. Why must soldiers obey their officers? Because an army is of no use without discipline. Why must subjects obey their Government? Because there would be no law or order if they did not. But obedience to God is the first law. If any man tells us to do wrong, we must disobey, so that we may obey God. God's laws must come first.

112. Example is Better than Precept

A drill-sergeant teaches raw recruits their drill by example. He not only tells them what to do; he does it himself before them. They watch him "slope-arms", "stand-at-ease", "stand-at-attention", "right-turn", "left turn", "right-about-turn". They copy his movements. They learn by his example. In teaching anything, example is better than precept. A "Precept" is an order or command. But we learn to do a thing by watching someone do it. An example is better understood than a mere explanation. So it is in moral conduct. The example of a good man has more effect on us than good advice or grand sermons. The story of a brave deed makes us want to be brave ourselves. The life of some kind and unselfish person stirs us up to be kind and unselfish.

113. Health

Health is better than wealth. It is one of God's best gifts to us. But it can be easily lost. It seems natural to us to be well when we are young. We cannot think what illness is like. So we don't think much about our health. We are often careless about it. Without thinking we spoil our health by bad habits and doing silly things. When we have lost it we find its value. How can we keep our health? Only by knowing and obeying the laws of health. First, we must eat good, plain food. We must eat enough and not too much. Secondly, we must have plenty of fresh air. Thirdly, we must take regular bodily exercise. Fourthly, we must get enough sleep. "Early to bed and early to rise makes a man healthy." Fifthly, we must work. Lastly, we must avoid forming bad habits. So we can maintain it.

114. Selfishness

A certain amount of self-love is right and proper. Self-love and self-respect are like salt. They keep our moral nature clean and fresh, as salt keeps the sea. But selfishness is bad. Selfishness is self-love carried to excess. Selfishness is the root of all sin. All true religions teach "Islam"; that is, "submission" to the will of God. But selfishness is putting our own will first. The God of the selfish man is himself. True religion also teaches love — love to God and love to our fellowmen. But selfishness is opposite of love. A selfish man thinks only of his own happiness and success. Every sin is a form of selfishness. Pride, dishonesty, meanness, theft, cruelty, murder are all bitter fruits of selfishness. Selfishness is an ugly and hateful thing. And it leads to unhappiness. True happiness springs from unselfishness. We must try to forget ourselves, and think of others.

115. The Worth of a Good Character

Character is not the same as reputation. A man's reputation is what others think he is. A man's character is what he really is. It is his real moral condition, good or bad. What is the worth of having a good character? Compare good character with good health, happiness and wealth. Good health is a great blessing. So is happiness. So can wealth be. But are they worth more than a good character ?

If we can have all the four, we are blessed indeed. But suppose we can have only one. Which shall we choose ? Is it better to be a healthy villain, or a sick saint ? Is it better to be rich and wicked, or poor and good ? Is it better to be happy and bad, or sad and noble ? We know that good character is really worth all the rest. It is the best of all to be good, whatever else we may be.

116. More Haste, Less Speed

At first sight this proverb seems to make no sense. Surely haste and speed mean the same thing. Both mean swift movement. But "more haste, less haste"; or, "more speed, less speed", would be nonsense. But here speed, means something else. To "speed the parting guest" means to wish him a good journey. And the wish, "God speed you!" means "May God give you success!" The word "speed" in this proverb means success. That is, the more you hurry to finish a piece of work, the less successful you will be in doing it. So the proverb is a warning against impatience. To do anything well takes time, thought and patience. "Slow and steady wins the race". This is true in education. Some students want to fly before they have learnt to walk. Hurry in learning means scamped work. Learning is a slow and patient business.

117. Luck

Nothing really happens by chance. Everything has a cause. But we do not always know the cause. Something happens which we cannot explain. Then we say it happened by chance. We really mean that we do not know why it happened. When it benefits us, we say it is good luck. When it harms us, we say it is bad luck. Foolish people believe in "luck". They call men who succeed in life "lucky". They call men who fail "unlucky". They think certain things bring bad luck. They are frightened if the salt is upset towards them. They will not walk under a ladder. They are afraid of the number "13". They say it is an unlucky number. So they will not sleep in room number 13 in a hotel. Of course all this is pure bullshit. There is no such thing as luck or chance.

118. Lying

Why do people tell lies ? One reason is fear. A servant breaks something. He is afraid his master will punish him. So he tells a lie. He says another servant did it. It often takes courage to tell the truth. A liar is a coward. He hides behind a lie. But all lying is not due to fear. People often tell lies from greed, to get money. A shop-keeper lies about his goods. He says they are the best. They may be only second-rate. But he gets more money for them by lying. Some people of low birth pretend to be noble and rich. They tell lies to get into good society. Lying is a very bad habit. It may pay for a time. But in the end it brings shame and much sorrow. No one trusts a known liar. No one wants him as a friend. Telling the truth pays the best.

119. Birds of a Feather Flock Together

"Of a feather" means of the same kind. Birds of the same kind naturally flock together. Crows flock with crows; sparrows go with sparrows; parrots live with parrots. It is the same with people. Men are divided into nations. Each nation has its own language and customs. The people of one nation "flock together". Indians flock with Indians; Englishmen with Englishmen; Germans with Germans; Japanese with Japanese. People of the same nation are divided into classes. There are the rich, the middle-class and the poor. Rich people find friends in their own class. They do not mix much with the poor or the middle-class. People of the same class flock together. Then some men are good; others are bad. Some are honest and hard-working; others are lazy and dishonest. These classes will keep apart. "We can know a man by the company he keeps."

120. The Duties of a Citizen

The word "citizen" is used for the member of a city or a country. We can speak of London or Calcutta, or of a citizen of England or of India. What are the duties of a citizen to his city or country ? The first is loyalty. True patriotism means that in times of danger a citizen must support and fight for his fatherland. Secondly, obedience to the laws of his country and his city. He must have no sympathy with crime, which is a breach of the law. Thirdly, it is his duty to help the police in putting down crime and arresting criminals. Fourthly, he must take an intelligent interest in politics. He should have an opinion as to what is the best for his country. And he should do all in his power to get it carried out. He should serve his country in every way he can.

121. Two Sides to Every Question

Two knights once fought about a shield they found hanging from a tree.

One said it was gold. The other said it was silver. Afterwards they found they were both right, and both wrong. The shield was gold on one side, and silver on the other. So every question has two sides. Some see one side. Others see the other. It takes a broad-minded person to see both sides. For example, take politics. There are two political parties. One, the Conservatives, want to keep things as they are. They say change is dangerous. The other, the Progressives, want progress and reform. They say we cannot progress without change. Both are so far right. But each sees only one side of the question. We must have reform and progress. But we must not lose sight of what is good in the past. We want both sides — The Conservatives and the Progressives.

122. Playing the Game

"To play the game" is a sporting term. It means playing a game, or doing anything, in a sporting spirit. What is "the sporting spirit"? It is fair play and no favour; enthusiasm for the same; pluck; generosity to opponents; ability to take defeat well. A real sportsman will always play fair. He will take the game seriously, and is keen to win. But he will take no unfair advantage. He will play a losing game with pluck and patience. If he wins, he will be modest about his victory. If he loses, he is not cross or sulky. He will shake hands warmly with the winner. A true sportsman will "play the game" in life. At school he will not scamp his work. He will not use "cribs" and cram-books. He will not lie to shield himself. In business he will work hard to beat his rivals; but he will play fair. Playing the game stands for honour, loyalty and duty.

123. Experience – the Best Teacher

Experience does not teach everything. It does not teach history, geography, chemistry. What it teaches is the Art of Living. No one can teach this subject as well as experience. She is a strict teacher. She charges very high fees. She punishes faults very severely. But she teaches her lesson thoroughly. We could learn much from other people's experience. But as a rule we have to learn from our own. You warn a child against playing with fire. *Your* experience has taught you the danger. But the child does not believe you till he has burnt his fingers. Then he learns from his own experience. "A burnt child dreads the fire." So we have to learn from our own experience such old truths as — "Honesty is the best policy"; "All is not gold that glitters"; "No pains, no gains"; "A rolling stone gathers no moss".

124. Necessity is the Mother of Invention

Suppose we could get all we wanted from nature. We should not bother to invent anything. But we cannot. So we have been forced to invent things. When men were hunters, they had to invent tricks and traps for catching wild animals. In cold countries they had to invent clothes to keep warm. When they wanted to cross the sea, they had to invent boats and ships. When they wanted plants for food, they had to invent shades and ploughs to dig up the ground. When they had to fight wild beasts or foes, they invented weapons — swords, spears, bows and arrows and guns. In the same way the invention of writing and then of printing, was due to the necessity of spreading news and knowledge. So necessity is called the mother of invention. Invention is due to necessity. But now men also go on inventing new things for pleasure.

125. Akbar the Great

Akbar's father was Humayun, the Mughal Emperor. He died when Akbar was only thirteen. Akbar had to fight for his throne. He became emperor in 1556. Akbar was a great soldier. He conquered all northern India. But he was more than a fighter. He was a wise, just and great ruler. He had to govern people of different races and religions. He ruled with justice to all. He was very tolerant. He did not interfere with people's religion. In this way he won his subjects' hearts. He was not educated. He married a Hindu Rajput princess – Jodhabai. He could not read or write. But he liked hearing learned men talk. He was keen on education. He was himself a thinker. He was an earnest seeker after truth. He actually thought out a new religion. He called it *Din-i-Ilahi*. He thought it would unite his people. But it died with him. Akbar died in 1605. He was a great king.

126. Buddha

Buddha was one of the world's great religious teachers. His real name was Gautama Siddhartha. He was born in the year 563 B.C. He was born a prince. His father was the Raja of Kapilvastu. But he did not want to be a Raja. He wanted to find out the meaning of life. He left his palace as a young man. He went out to seek the truth. For years he lived a hard life of poverty. He went to many teachers. But they could not help him. At last the light came to him. He had been then thinking deeply under the Bodhi tree, near Gaya, in Bihar. He became the "Buddha", or "the enlightened one". He spent the rest of his life in teaching his gentle religion. He won many disciples. Before he died, his religion, called Buddhism, had spread far and wide. He was over eighty when he died.

127. Abraham Lincoln

Abraham Lincoln was born in 1809. He was a self-made man. His father was a poor farmer. Abraham worked first as a lumber-man or wood-cutter. But he wanted to get on. He learnt to read and write. He got a job as a clerk. Then he was a store-keeper and then a postmaster. He studied law in his spare time. He became a lawyer. He took up politics. Soon he was well-known as an orator. In 1860 he made a famous speech against slavery. At that time slaves were kept in the Southern States of America. The same year he was elected President of the United States. He had climbed from "Log-Cabin" to "White House". Then came the American Civil War. It was between the Northern States and the slave-owning Southern States. The Northern States won. Lincoln abolished slavery in America. Lincoln was a great and good man. He was the greatest American President.

128. Florence Nightingale

Florence Nightingale was born in 1820. She belonged to a rich family. She might have led the life of a lady of fashion. But she had better work to do. She devoted her life to nursing the sick. She was herself a born nurse. She was the first to train women as nurses. She won fame in the Crimean War (1854-1856). The wounded English soldiers were at first neglected. The medical arrangements were in a muddle. Doctors were left without proper medicines. Miss Nightingale went out with a band of trained nurses. She was an able woman of strong will. She had great energy. She was a fine organizer. She put everything right. It was hard work and took time. But she won in the end. She saved many precious lives. She went round the hospitals at night with a lamp to see that all was well. The soldiers called her "The Lady with the Lamp".

129. Edison

Thomas Alva Edison, the great American inventor, was born in 1847. He began life as a poor boy. He earned his living as a newsboy on railway trains. But in his off-time he played with chemicals. He educated himself. He got work in a telegraph office. In time he became a clever telegraph engineer. He saw how the telegraph could be improved. His improvements were accepted. His inventive genius was recognized. But he had a hard struggle. When he was twenty-two he won forty-thousand dollars for an invention. He rose to be the Superintendent of a New York Telegraph Company. At last he was able to start his own workshops at Menlo Park. There most of his best-known inventions were made. He invented the phonograph, which led to the gramophone. Our moving pictures are due to him. He greatly improved electric light. His inventions are almost countless.

130. Ashoka

Ashoka was the third ruler of the Mauryan Empire. He reigned from 272 to 221 B.C. He was a very wise good King. He hated war. His rule was a reign of peace. Ashoka was a Buddhist. His aim was to get "Dharma" (righteousness) into the hearts of his people. Dharma was — *reverence* to superiors; *kindness* to all living creatures; *truthfulness* in thought, word and deed. He sent out missionaries preaching this righteousness. They went all over India. He banned cruel sports and animal sacrifices. He had a strong sense of duty. He did not leave the rule of his kingdom to his officers only. The poorest could go to him direct. He gave justice to all. He was truly the father of his people. Ashoka was one of the wisest kings in the world's history. There are few in any country to compare with him.

131. Edward Jenner

Small-pox was once as bad in England as it is in India. Now it is unknown there. How was it got rid of in England? It was due to the work of a doctor called Edward Jenner. He was born in 1749. As a country doctor he began studying small-pox in 1775. He found that people who got cow-pox never got small-pox. Cow-pox was a cattle disease much milder than small pox. He made experiments. He discovered vaccination. Vaccination is injecting a person with the lymph of a cow suffering from cow-pox. He published his discovery in 1798. But he was laughed at. No one believed it. At last it was recognized by the doctors. Jenner died in 1823. In 1851 vaccination was made compulsory. The result is that there is no small-pox in England. Small-pox was got rid of in India in the same way.

132. Christopher Columbus

Columbus was an Italian. He was born at Genoa in 1435. He became a sailor. He made many voyages. He knew the earth was round. He got the idea of getting to India (in the east) by sailing west. People laughed at him. But he stuck to his point. He was a poor man. He had no money to buy ships and hire sailors. Nobody would help him. At last the King of Spain gave him three small ships and crews. In those days no one knew what was across the Atlantic Ocean. They thought it was all sea. Columbus set sail over an unknown sea. He sailed for over two months without seeing land. His sailors rebelled. But Columbus sailed on. At last they came to land. Columbus thought it was India. It was really a new world. Without knowing it, Columbus had discovered America. This was in 1492.

133. J. N. Tata

Jamsetjee Nusserwanji Tata was born in 1839. He died in 1904. He was a Parsee from Bombay. Tata was the greatest industrialist India has produced. He was an able businessman, and became very wealthy. But he was also a great philanthropist. He devoted much of his wealth to helping others. He was the founder of the Indian cotton industry. His Empress Mills was among the first. He built up other great businesses. The Tata Steel Works are well-known. And his Hydro-Electric Works is a big concern. Tata was greatly interested in education. He founded several scholarships for Indian students. Some were for study in India. Some were for study abroad. Tata was the founder of the Institute of Research at Bengaluru. He gave £ 200,000 to start it; and has given liberally since. He will always be remembered as a great benefactor. His family has carried on his work since his death.

134. Marconi

We owe the radio and the wireless to Guglielmo Marconi. He was born at Bologna in 1874. He became a student in the Bologna University. He took up electricity as his chief subject. The telegraph and the telephone were already in use. Message could be sent by electricity along copper wires. Macroni's idea was to find a way of sending message by electricity without wires. He made experiments in his garden. He found he could thus send a message two miles. He offered his discovery to the Italian Government. It was refused. The English

Government took it up. They let Marconi set up a wireless station in Cornwall. Steamers were fitted up with Marconi's wireless instruments. This was the beginning. It led to wireless telephony or "broadcasting". Now we can "listen in" to music and men speaking thousands of miles away. Marconi was a great inventor.

135. Shivaji

Shivaji was the real founder of the Maratha nation. He was born in 1627. His father, Shahaji Bhonsle, was a Maratha chief. But he owed most to his mother, Jijabai. She was a devoted Hindu. She brought him up in the strict Hindu faith. Shivaji became an enthusiastic follower of her religion. He was trained to be a ruler by a Brahmin called Dadoji. Shivaji set himself to unite all the Maratha tribes into one nation, with one faith. He first freed them from the Muslim state of Bijapur in 1662. He then entered into a long struggle with the Mughal Emperor, Aurangzeb. The war with the Mughal lasted a long time. But it ended in victory for Shivaji. The Marathas became independent. Shivaji was crowned as Chattrapati in 1674 at Raigarh. He reigned for six years, dying in 1680. Shivaji was bold, active and clever, in fighting and ruling. He was a national hero.

136. Sir Isaac Newton

Isaac Newton was a great scientist. He was born in 1642, and died in 1727. He discovered the law of gravitation. It was the falling of an apple in his garden that set him thinking. He was trying to find why the earth went round the sun, and the moon round the earth. He asked himself, "Why does an apple fall to the earth?" This led him to his great discovery. Newton also found out that white light is made up of seven colours. We see the colours in a rainbow. He also made many other discoveries. Newton was a very learned man. But he was very humble. Shortly before his death he said, "I seem to have been only like a boy playing on the seashore, and amusing myself in now and then finding a smooth pebble or pretty shell, while the great ocean of truth lay all undiscovered before me."

137. The Duke of Wellington

His name was Arthur Wellesley. He was born in 1769. He first came to notice as a soldier in India. He fought in the Maratha War, and won victories at Assaye and Argaum (1803). But his fame was won in the Peninsular War in Spain (1808-1813). He was sent with a small army to help the Spanish and the Portuguese. Spain had been invaded by Napoleon's French armies. He had a very hard task. Wellesley showed great military skill. He had great patience and determination. He fought on year after year. At last he won. The French were driven out of Spain. This was a great blow to Napoleon. Wellesley was made Duke of Wellington, as a reward for his great work. But he is best known as the victor of Waterloo. This great battle was fought in 1815. Napoleon was beaten. The long Napoleonic wars ended. Later Wellington was Prime Minister. He died in 1852.

138. Rammohan Roy

Raja Rammohan Roy was born in 1774. He was born a Brahmin, and died a Brahmin. But he was a religious reformer. He studied the Quran and the Christian Bible. He tried to find the good in all religions. To find out all about them he learnt Arabic, Hebrew, Persian, Sanskrit. He also knew Latin, Greek, French and English. So he was good at languages. He shocked strict Hindus by preaching against Sati. He was also against man having more than one wife. And he was in favour of the re-marriage of widows. Rammohan Roy is noted as the founder of a new religion. This he called the Brahmo-Samaj. This began in Kolkata in 1814. His followers believed in one God. It was a simple religion. He said that Hindus, Muslims, Christians, Jews and Buddhists could all join in this way to worship one God.

139. "Make Hay while the Sun Shines"

Life is a moving shadow and is sometimes in the sun and sometimes in the shade. The horizon of life is not swayed by fair weather at all times. It is at times interspersed with thunder and storm. It is, therefore, wise to take time by the forelock and make the best use of the opportunities that come our way. Just as a farmer does not let one sunny day slip away to dry his hay, similarly we should make the best use of good times. Those who miss such golden opportunities suffer an irreparable loss in the end. We should seize the opportunities while they are within our grasp and utilise them to our best advantage rather than shed helpless tears on a rainy day.

140. The Child is the Father of Man

Childhood shows the man as morning shows the day. The child of today is the father of tomorrow. He possesses the traits which develop along with his physical growth and manifest themselves in due course. Childhood is the most important stage of life and children should be brought up with utmost care and caution so as to help their innate capacities to blossom forth. It is out of this stuff that eminent educationists, scientists, artists, statesmen, etc., who are the salt of the earth, are born. Children are the real wealth of a nation and if they are well looked after, the future of the nation is secure, for the children of today are the citizens of tomorrow.

141. A Visit to a Market

One day I went to the supermarket. We were a party of four friends. We went on our bicycles. After paying fifty paisa each, we put our bicycles in the stand outside the market. When we entered we were surprised to see big shops with banners fluttering over them. These were the shops of foreign goods. First we went into the American Goods shop. There we saw a taperecorder, a cup made of cut-glass and sewing machines. Next, we saw huge machines run by electric power. Then we went into a German shop where we saw a human body. It was a man's skeleton made of glass. It also contained shops exhibiting huge machines, cloth, glass-ware and hard-ware. We were very pleased to see the market. It was now about 9 p.m. We were completely tired. So we came out, took our bicycles and returned home.

142. Scene of a Village in Flood

Shreerampur is a small village situated on the banks of the Jamuna. Its poverty and small stature is clear from its mud huts with thatched roofs and kachha street. In the year of Indian Independence, i.e., nineteen hundred and forty seven it was a victim of a severe flood that kept its people suffering for nearly a fortnight. With the setting in of rains, the Jamuna began to rise and soon its water spread to the right and left. Poor Shreerampur was the first to fall its prey. Very soon its fields were under the water and gradually houses were also inundated. The vast expanse of the muddy river carried away a large number of buffaloes, bullocks, cows, sheep and goats. From a distance the tops of huts and trees appeared like small islands on which could be seen a large number of hens, cocks and other birds taking shelter.

143. How I Pass my Time when I am not Busy in Studies

Gardening is my hobby and the small garden facing my house is the result of this very hobby. By sitting in the midst of the flowers of my garden, I get the joy of being in the company of the members of my family. The colour and smell amuses the mind and enlivens the atmosphere of the house. Gardening requires careful hard work. I lay the beds for flowers by mixing manure with the earth. Then everyday I water the plants and weed out the beds. I also take care that birds and insects do not spoil the plants when they are springing forth. In one corner, I have made a small rockery overgrown with cactus, several varieties of thorny plants. Gardening has made me know the names of a large number of plants. What a sense of self-importance I feel when others ask me about the flowers grown by me. One forgets all the cares and worries as one sits there.

144. An Evening Out for Shopping

Connaught Place is the best shopping centre in New Delhi. People come there for shopping. My sister was to be married. One day in the afternoon my parents along with my sister came out for shopping. We went to several shops dealing in sarees and while others were busy in making a selection, I enjoyed looking at the windows. How beautifully and tastefully the different material had been displayed. The Balujas and the Batas did not look like shops dealing in shoes but fairy lands in dream. After purchasing sarees and a few shoes, we went to Khadi Bhavan. It is really a very huge shop. There are numerous counters for different types of goods. As we were walking towards the Taxi, my sister's eyes fell on a number of boys selling small garlands and ringlets made of sweet smelling jasmine and bela flowers. She bought two—one for herself and the other for back home.

145. How I Got Drenched and Enjoyed the Rainy Day

It was a cloudy morning. The breeze sometimes brought wet and pleasant smell of rain from a distance. Black Clouds coursed across the threatening sky. Occasionally there was a rolling thunder accompanied by a flash of lightning. It was cloudy when we started from the school. But now it began to rain and rain heavily. There was no escape, no place of shelter. I thought of running and I ran towards the school bus at full speed. The rain pattered on my back and side. I was completely drenched, but I was running at full speed. As luck would have it, I lost my track and the next moment I was in mud, and I felt as if I was going to be sucked by the earth surrounding me. I did not know what to do. When I felt that I was out, half the road had been washed away and my school party was only a furlong more.

146. The Scene at a Hospital

My friend has been lying ill in the Civil Hospital for some time past. I learnt about his illness only a few days back and, therefore, I decided to go and look him up. When I reached the hospital I found it a huge building consisting of several wings with a clock in the middle. The whole approach to the hospital was full of people waiting to be examined or waiting to see their relatives. When I entered the hospital through a big hall I found that there were a large number of rooms on the left and the right. The rooms were neat and tidy and there were separate arrangements for out-door and in-door patients. In the corridors of the hospital there was a great bustle and activity. Doctors and nursing sisters in their white uniforms were moving up and down. At a short distance, there was an operation theatre, fitted with the most modern appliances. Outside the operation theatre there was a set of stretchers and wheeled chairs. On enquiry I learnt that this was the Casualty Ward where those who are victims of accidents are treated.

147. Why I Enjoy Taking Part in a School Play

It was the last performance of our School Play. We had performed thrice prior to this and each time we had received a thunderous ovation. The news had spread around our city that the St. Xavier play was the thing to see and so we naturally had a House Full. The play was titled "Ali Baba and the Forty thieves", and the boys who represented the "Thieves" resembled in every way their part. But the boys who stole the show were those that took the parts of the "Dancing Girls". They were simply wonderful. As the "Finale" came to an end, a deafening applause emerged from the audience. Some stood up and cries of "encore" filled the hall. We sang the finale again but still the crowd would not let us go. One can imagine our feelings at this moment. We felt like Kings in a moment of triumph. The closing number was repeated two more times before the audience was satisfied.

148. Pleasures of Reading

Of all the amusements which can possibly be imagined for a hard-working man, after his daily-toil, there is nothing like reading an entertaining book. It calls for no bodily exertion, of which he has had enough. It transports him to a livelier and more interesting scene; and while he enjoys himself there, he may forget the evils of the present moment. Nay, it accompanies him to his next day's work, and if the book, he has been reading be anything above the very idlest and lightest, it gives him something to think of, besides the drudgery of his everyday occupation. If I were to pray for a taste which should stand me in good stead, under every variety of circumstances, and be a good source of happiness and cheerfulness through life, it would be a taste for reading. Give a man, this taste and the means of gratifying it and you can hardly fail to make a man happy, unless indeed you put into his hands a most perverse selection of books.

149. A Walk Through a Garden

Yesterday we went for a walk in the Company Garden. On all sides were green trees and flowering plants. The flowers presented a scene of colourfulness and we felt like plucking them. The rose bed was specially very attractive. In certain bushes the Birds were making their nests and there were fountains running on all sides. The water of the fountains was sparkling in the bright sun-shine and the light breeze made the whole atmosphere very refreshing. We enjoyed ourselves and remained in the garden for quite some time. The velvet like looking grassy plots were a special charm and we took out our shoes and played on the lawns. A walk through a garden is always good for health and mind.

150. A Railway Accident

Nowadays we often hear about the accidents on the railway. Only last night I was an eye witness to an accident on the Ambala-Kalka line. I was travelling by the Kalka mail and I was fast asleep when I heard a crash which woke me up with a jerk. The train had come to stop and the pitch dark of the night was full of crying and shouting. The Guard could be seen moving with his lamp and it took a few minutes before we came to realize that our train had collided with a goods-train coming from the opposite direction. The two engines had been badly damaged and the drivers of the ill-fated trains had been killed. One must be careful while driving a train at night. I shall not forget this event in my life.

NOTES

NOTES